Physical Characteri
Chinese Cre:
(from The Kennel Club bi

Tail: Set high, carried up or out when in motion. Long and tapering, fairly straight, not curled or twisted to either side, falling naturally when at rest.

Body: Medium to long. Supple. Chest rather broad and deep, not barrel-ribbed. Breast bone prominent. Brisket extending to elbows; moderate tuck-up.

Hindquarters: Rump well rounded and muscular, loins taut, stifles firm and long, sweeping smoothly into the well let down hocks.

Colour: Any colour or combination of colours.

Size: Ideal height in dogs: 28–33 cms (11–13 ins) at withers; bitches: 23–30 cms (9–12 ins) at withers. Weight varies considerably, but should not be over 5.4 kgs (12 lbs).

Feet: Extreme hare-foot, narrow and very long, with unique elongation of small bones between joints, especially in forefeet, which almost appear to possess an extra joint.

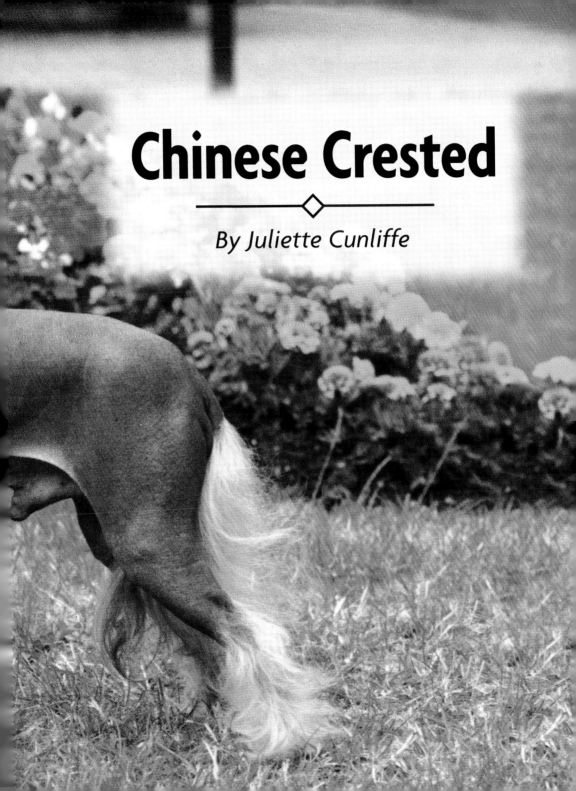

Chinese Crested

◇

By Juliette Cunliffe

CONTENTS

PUBLISHED IN THE UNITED KINGDOM BY:

INTERPET
PUBLISHING
Vincent Lane, Dorking, Surrey RH4 3YX England

ISBN 1-903098-94-7

PHOTOGRAPHS BY ISABELLE FRANÇAIS AND CAROL ANN JOHNSON
with additional photos by Norvia Behling, TJ Calhoun, Carolina Biological Supply, Doskocil, James Hayden-Yoav, James R Hayden, RBP, Bill Jonas, Dwight R Kuhn, Dr Dennis Kunkel, Mikki Pet Products, Phototake, Jean Claude Revy and Dr Andrew Spielman.
Illustrations by Patricia Peters.

The publisher wishes to thank Arlene Butterklee, Cindy Kumpfbeck, Mrs A and Miss T McGuigan, Carol and Paul Mount, Sande Weigand and the rest of the owners of the dogs featured in this book.

Speculation, fiction and novelty abound in
the history of the Chinese Crested and the
other hairless breeds.

History of the
CHINESE CRESTED

ORIGIN OF THE BREED

If there were a simple answer to where the Chinese Crested actually originated, undoubtedly many authors would be very happy. However, the Chinese Crested's history is a matter that has been the subject of speculation and debate, with almost more fiction than fact in its background.

The breed is certainly a distinctive one, but there are other hairless breeds, and the histories of various similar breeds may have been confused. The Chinese Crested, as we know it today, appeared in China's written history as long ago as the 13th century. Indeed, it is probable that the breed existed in that country long before then. Chinese seafarers and traders visited many places on their travels, and hairless dogs have since appeared in many of their ports of call. Hairless dogs were certainly also mentioned in the chronicles of Christopher Columbus and the other conquistadors.

It is possible that such dogs were kept on ships in order to control vermin, though, unhappily, they might also have been a source of food. Hairless dogs were undoubtedly found both in Asia and in Africa during the 18th and 19th centuries. However, a similar dog was also found in Mexico and in Central and South America in the 16th century. This dog was known as the Xoloitzcuintli, and is still known by that name or, alternatively, as the Mexican Hairless. This is registered as a different breed from the Chinese Crested. While there are obvious similarities between the two breeds, there are indeed differences. Even within the breed, Xoloitzcuintli vary tremendously in size.

An important question arises, though, about whether the

THE CHINESE CRESTED IN ART

There are several examples of the Chinese Crested Dog's appearance in works of art. Going back to the 15th century, a painting by Gerrard Davies entitled *Christ Nailed to the Cross* includes a hairless dog very similar to the Chinese Crested breed we know today.

Another painting of note is one painted by Jacques Laurent Agasse (1767–1849). This depicts a male Crested, clearly of the deer type. As with some of the engravings found in 19th-century canine works, the dog shown in the painting would not find himself out of place in today's show ring.

A modern Xoloitzcuintli, also known as the Mexican Hairless.

Illustration of a Chinese Crested in the early 19th century. The Crested was cited as 'one of the most unusual in appearance' among the hairless breeds found in various parts of the world at that time.

BRAIN AND BRAWN

Since dogs have been inbred for centuries, their physical and mental characteristics are constantly being changed to suit man's desires for hunting, retrieving, scenting, guarding and warming their masters' laps. During the past 150 years, dogs have been judged according to physical characteristics as well as functional abilities. Few breeds can boast a genuine balance between physique, working ability and temperament.

Chinese obtained their dogs from the Central and South American regions, or whether seafarers took along their own Chinese dogs to those lands, using them there for trade and barter. Perhaps one day the facts will be discovered but, to date, there is no conclusive evidence one way or the other.

THE NINETEENTH CENTURY

The first Chinese Crested Dogs in Britain, brought to the country in the 1860s, were placed in zoological collections and no serious attempt was made to breed from

An engraving of a Chinese Crested Dog in the 19th century.

Engraving entitled 'Hairless Dog' from _A Book of Beasts and Birds_, published in 1893.

in 1866 and was the only surviving puppy from a litter of six. When the book was written, she had never been bred from due to the difficulty in finding a suitable male 'of the same strain.' Because of its very affectionate disposition, it was believed that, if the breed could be developed, it

---

HAIRLESS BREEDS

There are many other hairless breeds of dog besides the Chinese Crested. Over the span of time these have included the Abyssinian or African Sand Dog, African Elephant Dog, Buenos Aires Hairless, Guatemalan Hairless, Inca Orchid, Nubian Dog, Peruvian Hairless, Small African Greyhound, Turkish Hairless, Xoloitzcuintli or Mexican Hairless and Zulu Sand Dog.

---

them; instead, they were treated as fascinating novelties. In the book _Dogs of the British Isles_, published in 1867, we read that the variety of Chinese dog furnished with a crest and tufted tail was by no means common. The dog's skin was described as spotted, and it was estimated that there were between 12 and 18 hairs on the surface of the body, thus making the tufts on the two extremities even more remarkable. It is interesting that 19th-century illustrations show the Chinese Crested with no tufts of longer hair on the feet. Indeed, most pictures of such dogs in the 1800s showed no hair in this area.

The bitch portrayed in _Dogs of the British Isles_ was two years old

would please many as something of a 'novelty pet.'

Several early canine writers maintained that the Chinese Crested Dog was the same dog as

the African Sand Dog and the hairless dogs of both Mexico and Japan. However, they did comment that the Chinese Crested had to have a crest on the top of the head and on the tail, something not common to all such breeds. The African Sand Dog also had a crest but, at least in those exhibited, it was shorter and much harsher than those of the Chinese Crested.

THE EARLY TWENTIETH CENTURY

As the 20th century turned, we find the Chinese Crested described as an 'outlandish' breed of 'rather a rare sort.' Charles Henry Lane, a prominent show judge of the day, wrote that, although he had judged Foreign Dog classes at all of the leading shows, there had been very few specimens of this scarce breed exhibited under him.

The best Chinese Crested that Lane had ever seen was called Chinese Emperor, owned by Mr W K Taunton. He commented that the tuft of stiffish hair, either on the forehead or above it, was usually nearly white or a 'whitey brown' in colour, as was the tuft on the top end of the tail. In shape and style of body, the breed resembled a coarse, strong Italian Greyhound, but the Chinese Crested nearly always gave one the impression of its being adversely affected by the cold! In

> ## GENUS *CANIS*
> Dogs and wolves are members of the genus *Canis*. Wolves are known scientifically as *Canis lupus* while dogs are known as *Canis domesticus*. Dogs and wolves are known to interbreed. The term *canine* derives from the Latin derived word *Canis*. The term 'dog' has no scientific basis but has been used for thousands of years. The origin of the word 'dog' has never been authoritatively ascertained.

Lane's view, this was not a breed suitable for the climate of Britain, unless in what he termed 'favourable circumstances,' and he had never heard of their being used for anything other than companions and pets.

In 1903, W K Taunton, writing in the book *British Dogs* by Drury, referred to Chinese Cresteds as terriers. He commented on the great variance in size within the breed, from 4.5 kgs (10 lbs) up to as much as 11.5 kgs (25 lbs), saying that in recent years he had found them of varying quality. He even advised prospective purchasers to make certain that they were buying a genuine hairless dog, not a terrier without hair. In his opinion, any appearance of tan on the legs and feet

H C Brooke's Mexican Hairless, Paderewski Junior, circa 1907. This dog was famous during his time for his intelligence and hunting ability.

suggested a cross of Black-and-Tan Terrier blood.

The Chinese Crested's skin was expected to be bluish in colour, resembling the colour of an elephant's hide. Although the skin was frequently mottled, this apparently was not considered correct at that time.

Perhaps the temptation of the 19th- and early 20th-century canine writers to link the hairless breeds with terriers had something to do with the dogs' gameness. In 1904, Herbert Compton treats readers of his book *The Twentieth Century Dog* to what he calls 'a not altogether happy-looking little animal' by the name of Paderewski Junior, a Mexican Hairless. He and his

An engraving from 1791 of the 'Naked Turkish Dog.'

father, Hairy King (who was, incidentally, captioned 'Chinese Crested Dog' in the 1903 *British Dogs*), were splendid ratters, and Junior was considered exceptionally intelligent and game. He would hunt rabbits in company with a pack of Beagles, and could face gorse as well as, if not better than, the hounds.

Like the breed's ancestors, today's Chinese Crested is a remarkable sight.

The Zulu Sand
Dog, circa 1907.

By 1907 the Chinese Crested, along with other hairless breeds, still created some attention in canine publications; these dogs were, after all, something of a curiosity. The size of hairless dogs in Britain varied between as little as 2 kgs (around 4 to 5 lbs) to as much as 11.5 kgs (25 lbs). There were two types. One was built along the lines of the Manchester Terrier, sometimes attaining the racy fineness of a Whippet, while the other was short-legged and cloddy. The latter was said to be 'decidedly unpleasant in appearance; its bareness giving the impression of disease, added to which it was prone to ungainly obesity.' It was, however, recognised that some specimens were very active and remarkably intelligent.

TEETH IN HAIRLESS BREEDS

Even during the breed's early recognition in Britain, it was noted that the dentition of Chinese Crested Dogs was abnormal and imperfect. Darwin had said that, in most animals, the teeth and horns had some relation to growth or absence of hair. Bald mammals seldom had large horns or tusks, while long-coated ones, such as Highland cattle, wild boars and even the hairy mammoth, were remarkable for their horns or tusks.

DID YOU KNOW?
Dating back to the fifteenth century, five Chinese Crested Dogs were included in the inventory of wedding gifts.

The bluish skin colour, resembling that of an elephant's hide, was mentioned in early 19th-century descriptions of the Chinese Crested.

SKIN AND LACK OF COAT GROWTH

Many of the early authors who wrote about the hairless breeds considered that their countries' dry climates might have had some effect at least in producing dogs without hair. The dogs' skin was usually extremely delicate and, unless smeared with grease, blistered in the summer if exposed to the sun.

By the early 1930s, one notable canine encyclopaedia said that hairless dogs could only be looked upon as 'freaks' due to the absence of certain bodies in their blood. It was also noted that some of the dogs had top-knots, and an interesting comparison was drawn with the human race—also practically hairless, except for hair on the head where it, too, could grow to a considerable length.

HAIRLESS DOGS CROSSED WITH OTHER BREEDS

A century or more ago, perhaps for the sake of curiosity or perhaps because of the difficulty in finding compatible members of their own kind, several crosses were made between hairless dogs and other breeds.

A Fox Terrier bitch was once mated to Hairy King, apparently because her owner needed to use the bitch as a foster mother for Bull Terrier puppies. Of the puppies produced by the mating, several puppies looked like fair specimens of Fox Terrier, but two of them were especially weird-looking creatures. They had Fox Terrier heads, but were hairless. Their skin was mottled along the body to the hips where, on each side, was a tuft of hair about the size of a crown piece. The tail was bare from its root to the middle, but the end was like that of a Fox Terrier, and, while the legs were bare to the knee joint, the feet also resembled those of a terrier.

Not all Chinese Crested Dogs are hairless. The coated variety, known as the Powder Puff, is otherwise basically identical to the Hairless, with only minor differences.

A WORD ABOUT THE MEXICAN DOGS

The Mexican Hairless was usually of a uniform colour and, though some described it as being 'of greyhound type,' it was only about 8 kgs (18 lbs) in weight. The breed was said to have been used externally on humans to ease the symptoms of rheumatism and, unfortunately, also internally to allay the pangs of hunger! So clearly both the Chinese and the Incas included the canine species in their diets.

The hairless dogs of Mexico were good guards and also popular as pet dogs, having the advantage of being practically free from fleas.

THE CHINESE CRESTED IN AMERICA

In 1880 Ida Garret, a New Yorker, became interested in the Chinese Crested Dog. She became so enthusiastically involved with the breed that she not only bred and exhibited Chinese Cresteds but also wrote about them. By the 1920s, Debra Woods had also become involved with the breed, and these two ladies worked hard to promote the Chinese Crested in the USA.

Debra Woods kept a logbook of all of her own dogs, which she

No longer frowned upon by Chinese Crested fanciers, the Powder Puffs are essential members of the breed.

Whether Powder Puff or Hairless, the Chinese Crested can be seen in any colour or combination of colours. The skin of the Hairless is often mottled.

bred under the kennel name 'Crest Haven.' By the 1950s, this was sufficiently extensive for her to begin a registration service for the breed and to establish the American Hairless Dog Club. Following the death of Mrs Woods in 1969, the registry was taken over by Jo Ann Orlirk and then became the property of the American Chinese Crested Club, founded in 1979. It was not, however, until 1991 that the breed was officially recognised by the American Kennel Club.

DID YOU KNOW?

It is sometimes said that the crest of hair on top of the Chinese Crested Dog's head is reminiscent of a Chinese pigtail, as worn in the past by the men of China.

UK REGISTRATION AND RISE IN POPULARITY

We know that there had been Chinese and other hairless dogs in Britain before, but it was not until 1881 that the first Chinese Crested Dog was actually registered in Britain. At that time, there was attention paid by The Kennel Club to the two distinct types of Chinese Crested—'deer' and 'cobby'—the latter being heavier in body and bone than the former, which was, and indeed still is, racy and fine boned.

Although the breed had appeared in England in small numbers from time to time, it was 2 December 1965 that heralded the beginning of Britain's modern-day Chinese Crested Dogs. America's Debra Woods exported the bitch Alto to Mrs Ruth Harris of the Staround kennels in Britain. Alto arrived in whelp, but sadly her puppies did not survive. However, this reputedly sound bitch with erect ears was shown at Championship Shows in the Any Variety classes, and she was featured not only in the newspapers but also on television and radio.

The following year, Mrs Harris imported two bitches, Brittas and Eloa, and a dog, Nero, from the same source. In the late 1960s, other dogs and bitches came in from the Crest Haven kennels. In 1969, the popular entertainer Gypsy Rose Lee brought over

The large, high-set ears complement the breed's quizzical expression. Fringe on the ears, when present, adds to the Crested's elegance.

The variation in colour and mottling from dog to dog makes each Chinese Crested truly one-of-a-kind in looks.

parents can include coated puppies. It was clear that the Lee and Crest Haven lines, mated together, produced not only stronger animals, but also heavier crests and plumes. More and more people showed an interest in the breed, and soon demand outstripped supply.

The Chinese Crested is now fairly well-scattered in show rings across the globe, though numbers and quality vary from country to country. The breed was first imported to Australia in 1975; this country has had an ardent band of Chinese Crested followers ever since.

three Chinese Cresteds of different bloodlines from her own kennels.

More Chinese Cresteds were imported to Britain during the 1970s, but not all of these came from the USA. All were hairless, but litters sired by hairless

POWDER PUFFS

Although coated Chinese Crested Dogs, known as Powder Puffs, were known from the early days of the breed in Britain, for several years after the foundation of the Chinese Crested Dog Club in 1969 such specimens were frowned upon. Members of the club were actually asked neither to breed from them nor to register them with The Kennel Club. There was indeed much debate as to what should actually be done with them! Some thought it would be best to try to develop them as a separate breed, others believed it would be better to cull them.

Although Powder Puffs appeared in litters produced from two hairless parents, there was considerable difference in type

GYPSY ROSE LEE

Gypsy Rose Lee, the famous American singer, dancer and entertainer, was greatly involved with promoting the Chinese Crested breed throughout the world. Her sister had obtained a Chinese Crested from an animal shelter in Connecticut and presented the dog to Ms Lee in the 1950s. Many of today's dogs can be traced back to Ms Lee's breeding.

among the coated puppies produced. Some could be as tall as 43 cms (17 ins), while others were very small; yet others were of suitable size and quality to compete with the coated specimens of the breed found in the show ring today.

In the early 1970s at a breed club Annual General Meeting, it was passed that 'Hair on any other part of the body other than stated in the standard' was a disqualifying fault. But time has moved on—in the 1980s opinions were modified and the standard was changed so that now the Powder Puff is regularly exhibited alongside hairless dogs in the same class.

The Powder Puff's ears may be dropped or erect, while the ears of the Hairless must be erect. This Powder Puff shows erect ears with lovely black fringe.

Characteristics of the
CHINESE CRESTED

WHY THE CHINESE CRESTED?

This graceful, elegant breed is frequently described as a little prancing pony, or sometimes as a fawn in miniature. The Chinese Crested is a small dog, and the Hairless variety requires minimal coat care. The coated variety, called the Powder Puff, requires a little more grooming, but nothing like the amount of time one needs to devote to the heavily coated breeds such as the Shih Tzu and Lhasa Apso. In Britain, both Hairless and Powder Puff Chinese Crested Dogs are shown in the same classes and are judged by the same breed standard.

The appearance of the Hairless variety does not, understandably, appeal to everyone, but those who like the breed are usually head over heels about this fun-loving, affectionate companion.

PERSONALITY

This is a happy breed, one that should never be vicious, although it can be a little feisty and will not be put upon by other dogs. Tremendous fun around the home, the Chinese Crested usually enjoys the company of other pets and thoroughly enjoys family life,

Puppy meets cat! Although small, the Chinese Crested can certainly hold his own and usually gets on well with other family pets.

in which he participates enthusiastically. This is a breed that loves to be with its owners, whether inside or outside the house. With their skin that is warm to the

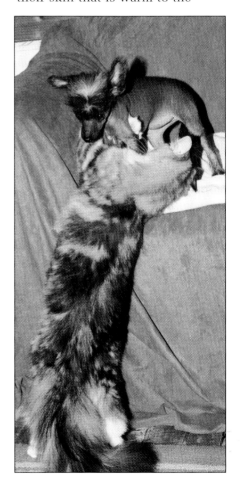

touch, more than a few enjoy acting as 'hot-water bottles' on cold nights! In the past it was claimed that the breed could 'cure' arthritis, though perhaps today that would be considered a little far-fetched.

The Chinese Crested is not a dog that should be left alone for long periods of time, for he enjoys company too much. When in the mood for love, he adores being cuddled and is affectionate in return. Due to their affectionate nature and intelligence, some Chinese Crested Dogs have been used in therapy work, especially in the USA.

This is an agile breed that thoroughly enjoys play, but its small size must be taken into consideration; excessive 'rough-and-tumble' is not advised. Like most other breeds of dog, the Chinese Crested can enjoy the company of children, but it is essential that small children are always supervised with dogs and that they are taught to treat them with respect.

Because the Chinese Crested can be rather shy, socialisation is very important. Without this, there is a danger of the Chinese Crested's becoming rather nervous and over-protective of his most treasured human friends. It is important, therefore, to devote plenty of time to the breed, which is exceptionally intelligent and is usually ready to learn basic

DID YOU KNOW?
The coated Chinese Crested, known as the Powder Puff, can be produced as the result of a mating of two Hairless dogs, or of a Hairless mated with a Powder Puff. Both of these combinations can produce either coat type. However, a Powder Puff mated to another Powder Puff will only produce its own kind.

obedience commands. Provided that training is made interesting, and that the dog can see a point in the exercise, training can be relatively easy. The breed can, though, be rather stubborn at times.

The Chinese Crested is viewed as somewhat of a primitive breed and, as such, they have a tendency to mark their territory just as their ancestors

Chinese Cresteds love to be with their owners wherever they go!

to use their barks, so firm control in this area from the outset is a wise thing. The Chinese Crested will always let its owners know when someone has arrived at the door, but will generally quieten down when the visitor has been welcomed.

PHYSICAL CHARACTERISTICS

Small, active and graceful dogs, their bone varies between fine and medium, for there are two distinct types. One is type is known as 'deer' and is racy and fine boned; the other is known as 'cobby' and is heavier in both bone and bodily structure.

Both types have a very distinctive extreme hare-foot, which should be long and narrow. There is a unique elongation of the small bones between the joints, so that the feet appear almost to have an extra joint, although actually they do not. The dog's nails are kept fairly long as well. The feet of the Chinese Crested have sometimes been likened to hands, for the dogs are quite capable of curling up their feet to grasp and hold objects, in a rather prehensile fashion.

With his slightly rounded and elongated skull, the Chinese Crested has cleanly chiselled cheeks that taper into the muzzle. The eyes are so dark as to appear black, and the nose is a prominent feature, being narrow in keeping with the muzzle.

did. This applies both to dogs and to bitches. They also make fairly good watchdogs and are not afraid

TAKING CARE

Science is showing that as people take care of their pets, the pets are taking care of their owners. A study in 1998, published in the *American Journal of Cardiology,* found that having a pet can prolong his owner's life. Pet owners generally have lower blood pressure, and pets help their owners to relax and keep more physically fit. It was also found that pets help to keep the elderly connected to their community.

'HOT-WATER BOTTLE'
The Hairless Chinese Crested has a body that is warm to the touch. Its temperature is 40 degrees Celsius, as opposed to 38–39 degrees, the temperature of most other breeds. It comes as no surprise, then, that the breed is sometimes deservedly known as a walking hot-water bottle.

SIZE
The size of the breed can vary quite considerably, both in height and in weight. Males should ideally measure 28–33 cms (11–13 ins) at the withers, while bitches are 23–30 cms (9–12 ins). In accordance with the variance in both height and bone structure, weight is variable, but should not exceed 5.4 kgs (12 lbs).

SKIN AND COAT
Another very obvious difference in the breed is that of coat, for two

DO YOU WANT TO LIVE LONGER?
If you like to volunteer, it is wonderful if you can take your dog to a nursing home once a week for several hours. The elder community loves to have a dog with which to visit, and often your dog will bring a bit of companionship to someone who is lonely or somewhat detached from the world. You will be not only bringing happiness to someone else but also keeping your dog busy—and we haven't even mentioned the fact that it has been discovered that volunteering helps to increase your own longevity!

types of coat can be produced in the very same litter. One type has a smooth hairless body, with hair on the feet, head and tail only; the other, known as the Powder Puff, has an undercoat with a soft veil of long hair, the veil coat being a distinct feature of this type.

On the Hairless dogs, the skin is fine-grained, smooth and warm to the touch. Perhaps surprisingly, it does not scratch easily. However, owners should be aware of the fact that the skin can burn in sunlight and, whatever the weather, a little baby oil, lotion or a suitable cream should be

applied to the skin to keep it soft and supple. One of the advantages of the naked variety is that it is highly unlikely to harbour fleas! There is also no doggy odour, nor indeed any dandruff, so this breed makes a good pet for a house-proud owner.

Although known as 'Hairless,' even the hairless dogs have some hair. This should be restricted to the tail, feet and head, where the crest ideally begins at the stop and tapers off down the neck. Although a long, flowing crest is preferred, a sparse one is accept-able. The plume on the tail is restricted to the lower two-thirds but, again, a sparse plume is acceptable. The coat on the feet is referred to as 'socks,' and these ideally should be confined to the toes and should never extend above the top of the pastern. In theory, Hairless Chinese Crested Dogs should have no hair on their bodies, but some do grow a minimal amount of hair. In this case, the small amount of body hair simply will need to be tidied up.

The Powder Puff coat on a five-month-old puppy.

The Powder Puff variety is the same dog as the Hairless variety other than in coat and in occasional minor differences in dentition, ear carriage and, according to some owners, personality.

COLOUR

Chinese Crested Dogs may be any colour or combination of colours, allowing for a wide range, both plain and spotted. Frequently, spotted dogs are pink all over when born, and spots begin to appear after about a week. The spots initially appear as pin-sized dots, gradually increasing with the progression of time. In summer, the colour has a tendency to deepen.

The variety of colours found in this very special little breed of dog include white, pink, blue and copper, among many others. A puppy that is born black may well turn out silver, white or even tri-

The Chinese Crested is not special ONLY for his looks. He's a small dog packed with personality, intelligence and affection.

coloured by the time he has reached maturity. In Powder Puffs the coat colour may change with maturity, sometimes becoming lighter with age.

TEETH

The Chinese Crested should have a strong jaw, with teeth closing in a scissor bite, meaning that the upper incisors closely overlap the lower ones. In Powder Puffs breeders expect full dentition, but Hairless Chinese Cresteds frequently have fewer teeth. Sometimes the canines face forward in the Hairless, in which case the teeth are known as 'tusks.' Hairless Chinese Crested Dogs typically have missing premolars.

HEART HEALTHY

The *Australian Medical Journal* in 1992 found that having pets is heart-healthy. Pet owners had lower blood pressure and lower levels of triglycerides than those who didn't have pets. It has also been found that senior citizens who own pets are more active and less likely to experience depression than those without pets.

The size, set and fringe of the Crested's ears add splendour to an already magnificent-looking breed.

TOENAILS
Toenails on Chinese Crested Dogs are kept moderately long, and on occasion a Hairless may have missing toenails.

EARS
The Chinese Crested's ears are large, but set low, with the highest point of the base being level with the outside corner of the eye. They stand erect on all Hairless Chinese Crested Dogs, giving a rather quizzical expression, especially when fully alert. Hairless dogs often have a fringe on their ears, adding to the breed's splendour, but lack of fringing is not considered a fault. The ears on the Powder Puff may also stand erect, but drop ears are also permissible in the coated variety.

TAILS
On both the Hairless and Powder Puff varieties, the tail is set high and, when the dog is in motion, carried up or out. When at rest, the long, tapering tail falls naturally, neither curled nor twisted to either side.

HEALTH CONSIDERATIONS IN THE BREED
In general, the Chinese Crested is a healthy breed. They are hardy little dogs, although, as has been

PECULIARITIES
In Chinese Crested Dogs, heat is released via sweat glands rather than by way of panting; panting is how most other breeds lower their temperatures when hot. Another rather unusual characteristic is that many act in a somewhat feline manner and, on occasion, clean themselves as a cat would.

mentioned, it is sensible to be aware of the potential danger of sunburn in hot weather. The Chinese Crested is a member of the Toy Group and, as such, can be prone to some of the medical problems encountered by other members of this group.

LEGG-CALVE-PERTHES DISEASE

Legg-Calve-Perthes disease, or necrosis of the femoral head, is believed to be hereditary, as it seems to be noticed more in some family bloodlines than in others. It occurs more frequently in smaller breeds of dog than in larger ones. Initial lameness slowly becomes worse, eventually

FREE WHELPERS

Unlike some of the more exaggerated breeds, the Chinese Crested is what is known as a 'free whelper.' Veterinary assistance is rarely required during the whelping process but, of course, as with any dog, complications can arise from time to time, so breeders should always be prepared as whelping time approaches.

BLOCK THE SUN!

Chinese Crested are more sensitive to solar damage than are most other breeds, due to their obvious lack of coat and pink skin pigmentation. Though white-coated dogs prove to be equally at risk, the Chinese Crested has the advantage of having nice smooth skin on which to apply a sunscreen (never less than SPF 15). Symptoms of sunburn include skin that is tender and painful, redness and, in bad cases, blisters and ulceration. Be certain to protect the dog's most sensitive body parts and avoid the dog's being outdoors during peak sun hours.

causing the dog to carry the affected limb. With time, due to disuse, the muscles of the thigh and upper leg disappear and the head of the femur becomes distorted. This condition can encourage further joint pain and osteoarthritis. Clearly, veterinary advice should be sought at the first sign of lameness.

PATELLAR LUXATION

A problem from which some Chinese Crested Dogs can suffer is patellar luxation, which is trouble with the knee joints. A sign of this

PHOTO BY M A STEVENSON, DVM, AND THE JOURNAL OF THE AMERICAN VETERINARY MEDICINE ASSOCIATION

X-ray diagnosis of elbow displasia in a three-and-a-half-year-olad dog.

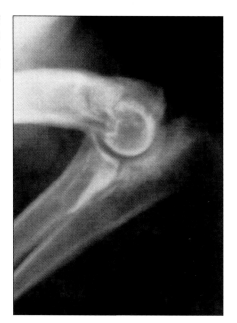
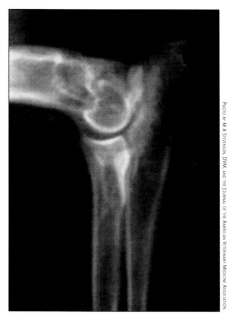

is when the dog limps or carries one leg off the ground when running. The dog does this because a bone has slipped out of position, due either to injury or to poor alignment. It is important that a dog so affected is not allowed to become overweight, as this is likely to exacerbate the problem.

Many dogs with patellar luxation live with the problem without experiencing pain, but sometimes surgery is necessary. A veterinary testing procedure is available.

PROGRESSIVE RETINAL ATROPHY (PRA)

Although there appears to be no evidence of progressive retinal atrophy in the breed in Britain, breeders of Chinese Cresteds in some countries have their stock tested for PRA. This is an hereditary eye disease that results in eventual blindness, caused by a breakdown of cells in the retina. The onset of blindness is usually slow, and an affected dog experiences no pain.

OTHER EYE PROBLEMS

Some Chinese Cresteds are known to suffer from 'dry eye' (keratoconjunctivitis sicca), usually caused by a lack of tear production. There can be several reasons for this: lack of nerve stimulation near the lachrymal glands, malfunction of the tear glands or blockage of tear ducts.

In dogs thus affected, the eyes themselves are dry and lack their usual lustre. This problem can be controlled with the application of artificial 'tears,' but veterinary guidance should always be sought to determine the cause.

Some owners shave the eyelashes of their Chinese Crested Dogs, and these, too, can cause a problem as they grow back in.

PROBLEMS WITH HAIR FOLLICLES

True hairless dogs can get little 'hooks' in the skin, caused by the hairs' being unable to grow. Should this happen, the little 'hooks' will need to be taken out.

TOOTH LOSS

The Chinese Crested has a tendency to lose its teeth sooner than many other breeds, and this is especially prevalent in the Hairless variety. This gives

owners all the more reason for always carefully checking their dogs' teeth, keeping them as clean as possible.

ACNE AND OTHER SKIN PROBLEMS

Hairless Chinese Crested Dogs are susceptible to having blackheads and pimples. It is therefore essential that their skin is kept thoroughly clean, and routine grooming is important, despite their lack of coat.

Some suffer from acne during the equivalent of a human's 'teenage' stage of development, but they usually grow out of it. Veterinary assistance can be of help, and some owners have found that a five- or six-week course of antibiotics can solve the problem. Clearly, though, it is always wiser to find solutions without the use of antibiotics if at all possible.

WOOL AND LANOLIN ALLERGIES

A high proportion of Chinese Crested Dogs is allergic to woollen items or products that contain wool. For this reason, woollen sweaters and the like cannot be used for this breed. Likewise, one should be aware of bedding products; those such as sheepskin bed liners must be avoided.

Lanolin, or products containing lanolin, have also been known to create an allergic reaction in this breed.

Cresteds don't mind cotton against their skin, but avoid hugging your dog when you're wearing wool.

The breed standard for the Chinese Crested Dog is set down by The Kennel Club and, like standards for other breeds, can be changed occasionally. Such changes come about usually with guidance from experienced people from within the breed clubs, but it should be understood that, in Britain, The Kennel Club has the final word as to what is incorporated and in what manner.

All breed standards are designed effectively to paint a picture in words, though each reader will almost certainly have a slightly different way of interpreting these words.

When one looks back to the early days and reads Britain's Interim Breed Standard for the Chinese Crested, one can see that today's recognised standard is more greatly detailed. A temperament clause has been written in, as well as an explanation of the two different types, 'deer' and 'cobby.' One will notice also that the Powder Puff variety was not recognised in the early standard. In addition, the head is now more fully described, as is the tail, and height range has been included, making this a much more useful and comprehensive standard for

those interested in the breed.

However, to fully comprehend the intricacies of a breed, reading words alone is never enough. It is just as essential for devotees to watch Chinese Crested Dogs being judged at shows and, if possible, to attend seminars at which the breed is discussed. This enables owners to absorb as much as possible about the breed they love so much. 'Hands-on' experience, providing an opportunity to assess the structure of dogs, is always valuable, especially for those who hope ultimately to judge the breed. However familiar one is with the breed, it is always worth refreshing one's memory by re-reading the standard, for it is sometimes all too easy to overlook, or perhaps conveniently forget, certain features.

A breed standard undoubtedly helps breeders to produce stock that comes as close as possible to the recognised standard, and helps judges to know exactly what they are looking for in the breed. This enables a judge to make a carefully considered decision when selecting the most typical Chinese Crested Dog present to head his line of winners.

THE KENNEL CLUB STANDARD FOR THE CHINESE CRESTED DOG

General Appearance: A small, active and graceful dog; medium- to fine-boned, smooth hairless body, with hair on feet, head and tail only; or covered with a soft veil of hair.

Characteristics: Two distinct types of this breed: Deer type, racy and fine boned, and Cobby type, heavier in body and bone.

Temperament: Happy, never vicious.

Head and Skull: Slightly rounded and elongated skull. Cheeks cleanly chiselled, lean and flat, tapering into muzzle. Stop slightly pronounced but extreme. Head

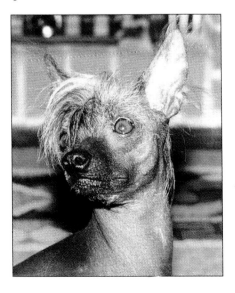

THE IDEAL SPECIMEN

According to The Kennel Club, 'The Breed Standard is the "Blueprint" of the ideal specimen in each breed approved by a governing body, e.g. The Kennel Club, the Fédération Cynologique Internationale (FCI) and the American Kennel Club.

The Kennel Club writes and revises Breed Standards taking account of the advice of Breed Councils/Clubs. Breed Standards are not changed lightly to avoid "changing the standard to fit the current dogs" and the health and well-being of future dogs is always taken into account when new standards are prepared or existing ones altered.'

Head study of an adult Chinese Crested bitch, showing alert expression, smooth skin, chiselled cheeks, prominent nose and long, graceful neck.

smooth, without excess wrinkles. Distance from base of skull to stop equal to distance from stop to tip of nose. Muzzle tapering slightly but never pointed, lean without flews. Nose a prominent feature, narrow in keeping with muzzle. Any colour nose acceptable. Head presenting graceful appearance, with alert expression. Lips tight and thin. An ideal crest begins at the stop and tapers off down neck. Long and flowing crest preferred, but sparse acceptable.

Eyes: So dark as to appear black. Little or no white showing. Medium size. Set wide apart.

Ears: Set low: highest point of base of ear level with outside corner of eye. Large and erect, with or without fringe, except in Powder Puffs where drop ears are permissible.

Mouth: Jaws strong, with perfect, regular scissor bite, i.e. upper teeth closely overlapping lower teeth and set square to the jaws.

Neck: Lean, free from throatiness, long and sloping gracefully into strong shoulders. When moving, carried high and slightly arched.

Forequarters: Shoulders clean, narrow and well laid back. Legs long and slender, set well under body. Elbows held close to body. Pasterns fine, strong, nearly vertical. Toes turned neither in nor out.

Body: Medium to long. Supple. Chest rather broad and deep, not barrel-ribbed. Breast bone prominent. Brisket extending to elbows; moderate tuck-up.

Hindquarters: Rump well rounded and muscular, loins taut, stifles firm and long, sweeping smoothly into the well let down hocks. Angulation of the rear limbs must be such as to produce a level back. Hind legs set wide apart.

Feet: Extreme hare-foot, narrow and very long, with unique elongation of small bones between joints, especially in forefeet, which almost appear to possess an extra joint. Nails any colour, moderately long. Socks ideally confined to toes, but not extending above top of pastern. Feet turning neither in nor out.

Tail: Set high, carried up or out when in motion. Long and

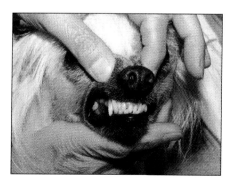

Adult Hairless displaying scissor bite. Powder Puffs must have full dentition, while Hairless frequently do not.

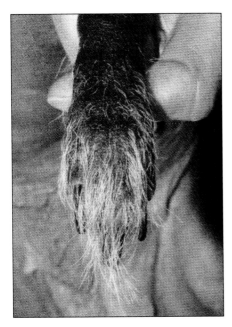

Size: Ideal height in dogs: 28–33 cms (11–13 ins) at withers; bitches: 23–30 cms (9–12 ins) at withers. Weight varies considerably, but should not be over 5.4 kgs (12 lbs).

Faults: Any departure from the foregoing points should be considered a fault and the seriousness with which the fault should be regarded should be in exact proportion to its degree.

Note: Male animals should have two apparently normal testicles fully descended into the scrotum.

An excellent illustration of the shape of the Crested's foot, which is narrow and very elongated. The foot is usually covered more profusely with hair.

tapering, fairly straight, not curled or twisted to either side, falling naturally when at rest. Plume long and flowing, confined to lower two-thirds of tail. Sparse plume acceptable.

Gait/Movement: Long, flowing and elegant with good reach and plenty of drive.

Coat: No large patches of hair anywhere on body. Skin fine-grained, smooth, warm to the touch. In Powder Puffs coat consists of an undercoat with soft veil of long hair, veil coat a feature.

Colour: Any colour or combination of colours.

BREEDING CONSIDERATIONS

The decision to breed your dog is one that must be considered carefully and researched thoroughly before moving into action. Some people believe that breeding will make their bitches happier or that it is an easy way to make money. Unfortunately, indiscriminate breeding only worsens the rampant problem of pet overpopulation, as well as putting a considerable dent in your pocketbook. As for the bitch, the entire process from mating through whelping is not an easy one and puts your pet under considerable stress. Last, but not least, consider whether or not you have the means to care for an entire litter of pups. Without a reputation in the field, your attempts to sell the pups may be unsuccessful.

Before reaching the decision that you definitely want a Chinese Crested puppy, it is essential that you are fully clear in your mind that this is absolutely the most suitable breed, both for you and for your family. You should have done plenty of background 'homework' on the breed, and preferably have visited a few shows at which the breed has been exhibited. This will have provided you with the opportunity to see the dogs with their breeders, owners and handlers, and you hopefully will have had a chance to see not only Hairless and Powder Puffs but also dogs of both cobby and deer type. These things are important, for you may decide that you have a preference,

> **PUPPY APPEARANCE**
> Your puppy should have a well-fed appearance but not a distended abdomen, which may indicate worms or incorrect feeding, or both. The body should be firm, with a solid feel. The skin of the abdomen should be pale pink and clean, without signs of scratching or rash. Check the hind legs to make certain that dewclaws were removed, if any were present at birth.

especially where coat is concerned. Dog shows can be good opportunities to talk with owners and breeders; most will be happy to answer your questions provided you approach them when they are not busy or awaiting a turn in the ring.

Remember that the dog you select should remain with you for the duration of its life, which is usually upwards of 13 years for a Chinese Crested, so making the right decision from the outset is of the utmost importance. No dog should be moved from one home to another simply because its owners were not considerate

Twelve-week-old Hairless puppy, on which the signature 'crest' is quite evident.

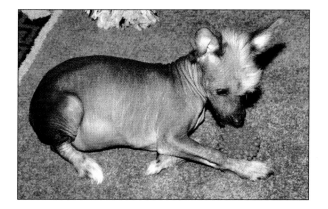

Two Hairless and a Powder Puff. Hairless-to-Hairless and Hairless-to-Powder Puff matings can produce either variety, while Powder Puff-to-Powder Puff will produce only coated pups.

enough to have done sufficient background research before selecting the breed and puppy.

Always be certain that the puppy you finally select has a seemingly sound personality; it should not be overly shy or aggressive. Never take pity on an unduly shy puppy, for in doing so you will be asking for trouble in the long run. Such a dog will likely have serious problems becoming socialised.

Puppies almost invariably look enchanting, but you must select one from a caring breeder who has given the puppies all the attention they deserve and who has looked after them well. They should already have been well socialised; this is likely to be apparent when you meet the litter.

The puppy you select should look well fed, but not pot-bellied, as this might indicate worms. Eyes should look bright and clear, without discharge. The nose should be moist, which is an indication of good health, but should never be runny. It goes without saying that there should certainly be no evidence of loose motions or of parasites. The puppy you choose should have healthy-looking skin or coat, depending upon whether you have selected a Hairless or a Powder Puff.

Gender will also play a role in your decision when selecting your puppy. Do you want a male or a female? In the Chinese Crested, males should be larger than

DID YOU KNOW?

You should not even think about buying a puppy that looks sick, undernourished, overly frightened or nervous. Sometimes a timid puppy will warm up to you after a 30-minute 'let's-get-acquainted' session.

where to find a puppy and what to look for. You should enquire about breeders who enjoy a good reputation in the breed. You are looking for an established breeder with outstanding dog ethics and a strong commitment to the breed. New owners should have as many questions as they have doubts. An established breeder is indeed the one to answer your four million questions and make you comfortable with your unique choice of the Chinese Crested. An established breeder will sell you a puppy at a fair price if, and only if, the breeder determines that you are a suitable, worthy owner of his dogs. An established breeder can be relied upon for advice, no matter what time of day or night. A reputable breeder will accept a puppy back,

females, and they tend to be a little more dominant. Some say that Chinese Crested males are more loving than bitches.

Something else to consider is whether or not to take out veterinary insurance. A veterinary surgeon's bills can mount up, and you must always be certain that sufficient funds are available to give your dog any necessary veterinary attention. Keep in mind, though, that routine vaccinations will not be covered by insurance.

SELECTING A BREEDER AND PUPPY

If you are convinced that the Chinese Crested is the ideal dog for you, it's time to learn about

PUPPY SELECTION

Your selection of a good puppy can be determined by your needs. A show potential or a good pet? It is your choice. Every puppy, however, should be of good temperament. Although show-quality puppies are bred and raised with emphasis on physical conformation, responsible breeders strive for equally good temperament. Do not buy from a breeder who concentrates solely on physical beauty at the expense of personality.

PREPARING FOR PUP

Unfortunately, when a puppy is bought by someone who does not take into consideration the time and attention that dog ownership requires, it is the puppy who suffers when he is either abandoned or placed in a shelter by a frustrated owner. So all of the 'homework' you do in preparation for your pup's arrival will benefit you both. The more informed you are, the more you will know what to expect and the better equipped you will be to handle the ups and downs of raising a puppy. Hopefully, everyone in the household is willing to do his part in raising and caring for the pup. The anticipation of owning a dog often brings a lot of promises from excited family members: 'I will walk him every day,' 'I will feed him,' 'I will house-train him,' etc., but these things take time and effort, and promises can easily be forgotten once the novelty of the new pet has worn off.

ownership. When choosing a breeder, reputation is much more important than convenience of location. Fortunately, the majority of Chinese Crested breeders are devoted to the breed and its well-being. The Kennel Club is able to recommend breeders of quality Chinese Cresteds, as can any local all-breed club or Chinese Crested club.

Once you have contacted and met a breeder or two and made your choice about which breeder is best suited to your needs, it's time to visit the litter. Keep in mind that it will take some time to locate a Chinese Crested litter and, once you do, you will probably have to put your name on a waiting list for a puppy. Sometimes new owners have to wait as long as two years for a puppy. If you are really committed to the breeder whom you've selected, then you will

without questions, should you decide that this is not the right dog for you.

Choosing a breeder is an important first step in dog

The whole family should take part in the selection process, from visiting the breeder to picking the perfect pup.

wait (and hope for an early arrival!). If not, you may have to resort to your second- or third-choice breeder. Don't be too anxious, however. If the breeder doesn't have a waiting list, or any customers, there is probably a good reason. It's no different than visiting a pub with no clientele. The better pubs and restaurants

DOCUMENTATION

Two important documents you will get from the breeder are the pup's pedigree and registration certificate. The breeder should register the litter and each pup with The Kennel Club, and it is necessary for you to have the paperwork if you plan on showing or breeding in the future.

Make sure you know the breeder's intentions on which type of registration he will obtain for the pup. There are limited registrations which may prohibit the dog from being shown, bred or competing in non-conformation trials such as Working or Agility if the breeder feels that the pup is not of sufficient quality to do so. There is also a type of registration that will permit the dog in non-conformation competition only.

On the reverse side of the registration certificate, the new owner can find the transfer section, which must be signed by the breeder.

YOUR SCHEDULE ...

If you lead an erratic, unpredictable life, with daily or weekly changes in your work requirements, consider the problems of owning a puppy. The new puppy has to be fed regularly, socialised (loved, petted, handled, introduced to other people) and, most importantly, allowed to visit outdoors for toilet training. As the dog gets older, it can be more tolerant of deviations in its feeding and toilet relief.

always have waiting lists—and it's usually worth the wait. Besides, isn't a puppy more important than a pint?

Since you are likely to be choosing a Chinese Crested as a pet dog and not a show dog, you simply should select a pup that is friendly, attractive and healthy. Chinese Crested litters average about five puppies, so selection is somewhat limited once you have located a desirable litter.

Breeders commonly allow visitors to see their litters by around the fifth or sixth week, and puppies leave for their new homes around the tenth to twelfth week. Breeders who permit their puppies to leave early are more interested in your pounds than in their puppies' well-being. Puppies

INSURANCE
Many good breeders will offer you insurance with your new puppy, which is an excellent idea. The first few weeks of insurance will probably be covered free of charge or with only minimal cost, allowing you to take up the policy when this expires. If you own a pet dog, it is sensible to take out such a policy as veterinary fees can be high, although routine vaccinations and boosters are not covered. Look carefully at the many options open to you before deciding which suits you best.

DID YOU KNOW?
Breeders rarely release toy puppies until they are around 10 to 12 weeks old, given their petite sizes. If a breeder has a puppy that is 12 weeks of age or older, it is likely well socialised and house-trained. Be sure that it is otherwise healthy before deciding to take it home.

need to learn the rules of the pack from their dams, and most dams continue teaching the pups manners and dos and don'ts until around the eighth week. Breeders spend significant amounts of time with the Chinese Crested toddlers so that the pups are able to interact with the 'other species,' i.e. humans. Given the long history that dogs and humans have, bonding between the two species is natural but must be nurtured. A well-bred, well-socialised Chinese Crested pup wants nothing more than to be near you and please you.

INHERIT THE MIND

In order to know whether or not a puppy will fit into your lifestyle, you need to assess his personality. A good way to do this is to interact with his parents. Your pup inherits not only his appearance but also his personality and temperament from the sire and dam. If the parents are fearful or overly aggressive, these same traits may likely show up in your puppy.

COMMITMENT OF OWNERSHIP

After considering all of these factors, you have most likely already made some very important decisions about selecting your puppy. You have chosen a Chinese Crested, which means that you have decided which characteristics you want in a dog and what type of dog will best fit into your family and lifestyle. If you have selected a breeder, you have gone a step further—you have done your research and found a responsible, conscientious person who breeds quality Chinese Cresteds and who should be a reliable source of help as you and your puppy adjust to life together. If you have observed a litter in action, you have obtained a firsthand look at the dynamics of a puppy 'pack' and, thus, you have learned about each pup's individual personality— perhaps you have even found one that particularly appeals to you.

However, even if you have not yet found the Chinese Crested puppy of your dreams, observing pups will help you learn to

ARE YOU A FIT OWNER?

If the breeder from whom you are buying a puppy asks you a lot of personal questions, do not be insulted. Such a breeder wants to be sure that you will be a fit provider for his puppy.

recognise certain behaviour and to determine what a pup's behaviour indicates about his temperament. You will be able to pick out which pups are the leaders, which ones are less outgoing, which ones are confident, which ones are shy, playful, friendly, aggressive, etc. Equally as important, you will learn to recognise what a healthy pup should look and act like. All of these things will help you in your search, and when you find the Chinese Crested that was meant for you, you will know it!

Researching your breed, selecting a responsible breeder and observing as many pups as possible are all important steps on the way to dog ownership. It may seem like a lot of effort...and you have not even taken the pup home yet! Remember, though, you cannot be too careful when it comes to deciding on the type of dog you want and finding out about your prospective pup's background. Buying a puppy is not—or should not be—just another whimsical purchase. This is one instance in which you actually do get to choose your own family! You may be thinking that buying a puppy should be fun—it should not be so serious and so much work. Keep in mind that your puppy is not a cuddly stuffed toy or decorative lawn ornament; rather, he is a living creature that will become a real member of your family. You will

'YOU BETTER SHOP AROUND!'

Finding a reputable breeder that sells healthy pups is very important, but make sure that the breeder you choose is not only someone you respect but also with whom you feel comfortable. Your breeder will be a resource long after you buy your puppy, and you must be able to call with reasonable questions without being made to feel like a pest! If you don't connect on a personal level, investigate some other breeders before making a final decision.

come to realise that, while buying a puppy is a pleasurable and exciting endeavour, it is not something to be taken lightly. Relax...the fun will start when the pup comes home!

Always keep in mind that a puppy is nothing more than a baby in disguise...a baby who is

PUPPY PERSONALITY

When a litter becomes available to you, choosing a pup out of all those adorable faces will not be an easy task! Sound temperament is of utmost importance, but each pup has its own personality and some may be better suited to you than others. A feisty, independent pup will do well in a home with older children and adults, while quiet, shy puppies will thrive in a home with minimal noise and distractions. Your breeder knows the pups best and should be able to guide you in the right direction.

virtually helpless in a human world and who trusts his owner for fulfilment of his basic needs for survival. In addition to food, water and shelter, your pup needs care, protection, guidance and love. If you are not prepared to commit to this, then you are not prepared to own a dog.

Wait a minute, you say. How hard could this be? All of my neighbours own dogs and they seem to be doing just fine. Why should I have to worry about all of this? Well, you should not worry about it; in fact, you will probably find that once your Chinese Crested pup gets used to his new home, he will fall into his place in the family quite naturally. However, it never hurts to emphasise the commitment of dog ownership. With some time and patience, it is really not too difficult to raise a curious and exuberant Chinese Crested pup to be a well-adjusted and well-mannered adult dog—a dog that could be your most loyal friend.

PREPARING PUPPY'S PLACE IN YOUR HOME

Researching your breed and finding a breeder are only two aspects of the 'homework' you will have to do before taking your Chinese Crested puppy home. You will also have to prepare your home and family for the new addition. Much as you would prepare a nursery for a newborn baby, you will need to designate a place in your home that will be the puppy's own. How you prepare your home will depend on how much freedom the dog will be allowed. Whatever you decide, you must ensure that he has a place that he can 'call his own.'

When you bring your new puppy into your home, you are bringing him into what will become his home as well. Obviously, you did not buy a puppy with the intentions of catering to his every whim and allowing him to 'rule the roost,' but in order for a puppy to grow into a stable, well-adjusted dog, he has to feel comfortable in his surroundings. Remember, he is leaving the warmth and security of his mother and littermates, as well as the familiarity of the only place he has ever known, so it is important to make his transition as easy as possible. By preparing a place in your home for the puppy, you are making him feel as welcome as possible in a strange new place. It should not take him long to get used to it, but the sudden shock of being transplanted is somewhat traumatic for a young pup. Imagine how a small child would feel in the same situation—that is how your puppy must be feeling. It is up to you to reassure him and to let him know, 'Little chap, you are going to like it here!'

Your puppy's crate will serve as a place of retreat... a home within his new home.

WHAT YOU SHOULD BUY

CRATE

To someone unfamiliar with the use of crates in dog training, it may seem like punishment to shut a dog in a crate, but this is not the case at all. Although all breeders do not advocate crate training, more and more breeders and trainers are recommending crates as preferred tools for show puppies as well as pet puppies. Crates are not cruel—crates have many humane and highly effective uses in dog care and training. For example, crate training is a very popular and very successful house-training method. In addition, a crate can keep your dog safe during travel and, perhaps most importantly, a crate provides your dog with a

PHOTO COURTESY OF DOSKOCIL

the type that you buy is up to you. It will most likely be one of the two most popular types: wire or fibreglass. There are advantages and disadvantages to each type. For example, a wire crate is more open, allowing the air to flow through and affording the dog a view of what is going on around him, while a fibreglass crate is sturdier. Both can double as travel crates, providing protection for the dog. The size of the crate is another thing to consider. Puppies do not stay puppies forever—in fact, sometimes it seems as if they

place of his own in your home. It serves as a 'doggie bedroom' of sorts—your Chinese Crested can curl up in his crate when he wants to sleep or when he just needs a break. Many dogs sleep in their crates overnight. With soft bedding and his favourite toy, a crate becomes a cosy pseudo-den for your dog. Like his ancestors, he too will seek out the comfort and retreat of a den—you just happen to be providing him with something a little more tidy than what his early ancestors enjoyed.

As far as purchasing a crate,

CRATE TRAINING TIPS

During crate training, you should partition off the section of the crate in which the pup stays. If he is given too big an area, this will hinder your training efforts. Crate training is based on the fact that a dog does not like to soil his sleeping quarters, so it is ineffective to keep a pup in a crate that is so big that he can eliminate in one end and get far enough away from it to sleep. Also, you want to make the crate den-like for the pup. Blankets and a favourite toy will make the crate cosy for the small pup; as he grows, you may want to evict some of his 'roommates' to make more room.

It will take some coaxing at first, but be patient. Given some time to get used to it, your pup will adapt to his new home-within-a-home quite nicely.

grow right before your eyes. It is best to purchase a crate that will accommodate your Chinese Crested both as a pup and at full size. As this is a small breed, you will not need a very large crate for the fully-grown Chinese Crested. The recommended size is 36 cms (14 inches) high, 36 cms (14 inches) wide and 51 cms (20 inches) deep, but you can purchase a crate that is a bit larger.

BEDDING

Veterinary bedding in the dog's crate will help the dog feel more at home, and you may also like to pop in a small blanket (not woollen). First, this will take the place of the leaves, twigs, etc., that the pup would use in the wild to make a den; the pup can make his own 'burrow' in the crate. Although your pup is somewhat removed from his den-making ancestors, the denning instinct is still a part of his genetic makeup. Second, until you take your pup home, he has been sleeping amid the warmth of his mother and littermates, and while a blanket is not the same as a warm, breathing body, it still provides heat and something with which to snuggle. You will want to wash your pup's bedding frequently in case he has a toileting 'accident' in his crate, and replace or remove any blanket that becomes ragged and starts to fall apart.

A remarkable gallery of Chinese Cresteds in their crates. Show dogs are always crate trained.

TOYS, TOYS, TOYS!

With a big variety of dog toys available, and so many that look like they would be a lot of fun for a dog, be careful in your selection. It is amazing what a set of puppy teeth can do to an innocent-looking toy, so, obviously, safety is a major consideration. Be sure to choose the most durable products that you can find. Hard nylon bones and toys are a safe bet, and many of them are offered in different scents and flavours that will be sure to capture your dog's attention. It is always fun to play a game of catch with your dog, and there are balls and flying discs that are specially made to withstand dog teeth.

Toys

Toys are a must for dogs of all ages, especially for curious playful pups. Puppies are the 'children' of the dog world, and what child does not love toys? Chew toys provide enjoyment for both dog and owner—your dog will enjoy playing with his favourite toys, while you will enjoy the fact that they distract him from chewing on your expensive shoes and leather sofa. Puppies love to chew; in fact, chewing is a physical need for pups as they are teething, and everything looks appetising! The full range of your possessions—from old tea towel to Oriental carpet—are fair game in the eyes of a teething pup. Puppies are not all that discerning when it comes to finding something literally to 'sink their teeth into'—everything tastes great!

Most toys are suitable for Chinese Crested puppies, but it is advised never to use cat toys, as a Crested will likely destroy them in no time. Breeders advise owners to resist stuffed toys, because they can become de-stuffed in no time. The overly excited pup may ingest the stuffing, which can be harmful and cause internal blockage.

Similarly, squeaky toys are quite popular, but must be avoided for the Chinese Crested. Perhaps a squeaky toy can be used as an aid in training, but not for free play. If a pup 'disembowels' one of these, the small plastic squeaker inside can be dangerous if swallowed. Monitor the

condition of all your pup's toys carefully and get rid of any that have been chewed to the point of becoming potentially dangerous.

Be careful of natural bones, which have a tendency to splinter into sharp, dangerous pieces. Also be careful of rawhide, which can turn into pieces that are easy to swallow and become a mushy mess on your carpet. It is never advised to allow your dog to chew on sticks, as they can be very dangerous.

If not given proper chew toys, your Crested will find things on which to chew, which could be dangerous to his teeth and his health.

LEAD

A nylon lead is probably the best option, as it is the most resistant to puppy teeth should your pup take a liking to chewing on his lead. Of course, this is a habit that should be nipped in the bud, but, if your pup likes to chew on his lead, he has a very slim chance of being able to chew through the strong nylon. Nylon leads are also lightweight, which is good for a young Chinese Crested who is just getting used to the idea of walking on a lead. For everyday walking and safety purposes, the nylon

PLAY'S THE THING

Teaching the puppy to play with his toys in running and fetching games is an ideal way to help the puppy develop muscle, learn motor skills and bond with you, his owner and master.

He also needs to learn how to inhibit his bite reflex and never to use his teeth on people, forbidden objects and other animals in play. Whenever you play with your puppy, you make the rules. This becomes an important message to your puppy in teaching him that you are the pack leader and control everything he does in life. Once your dog accepts you as his leader, your relationship with him will be cemented for life.

TEETHING TIP

Puppies like soft toys for chewing. Because they are teething, soft items like stuffed toys soothe their aching gums. Carefully supervise your pup with any stuffed or squeaky toy.

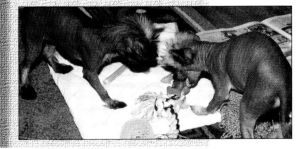

lead is a good choice. As your pup grows up and gets used to walking on the lead, you may want to purchase a flexible lead. These leads allow you to extend the length to give the dog a broader area to explore or to shorten the length to keep the dog near you.

COLLAR

Your pup should get used to wearing a collar all the time since you will want to attach his ID tags to it; plus, you have to attach the lead to something! A lightweight nylon collar is a good choice. Make certain that the collar fits snugly enough so that the pup cannot wriggle out of it, but is loose enough so that it will not be uncomfortably tight around the pup's neck. You should be able to fit a finger between the pup's neck and the collar. It may take some time for your pup to get used to

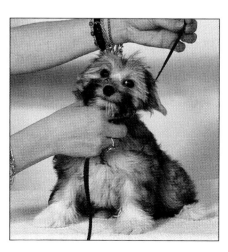

Accustom your pup to his lead and collar at an early age. Only a light nylon lead and collar are needed for a Chinese Crested.

wearing the collar, but soon he will not even notice that it is there.

FOOD AND WATER BOWLS

Your pup will need two bowls, one for food and one for water. You may want two sets of bowls, one for indoors and one for outdoors, depending on where the dog will be fed and where he will be spending time. Stainless steel or sturdy plastic bowls are popular choices. Plastic bowls are more chewable, but dogs tend not to chew on the steel variety, which can be sterilised. It is important to buy sturdy bowls since anything is in danger of being chewed by puppy teeth and you do not want your dog to be constantly chewing apart his bowl (for his safety and for your purse!).

CLEANING SUPPLIES

Until a pup is house-trained you will be doing a lot of cleaning. 'Accidents' will occur, which is acceptable in the beginning stages of toilet training because the puppy does not know any better. All you can do is be prepared to clean up any accidents as soon as they happen. Old rags, towels, newspapers and a safe disinfectant are good to have on hand.

BEYOND THE BASICS

The items previously discussed are the bare necessities. You will

CHOOSE AN APPROPRIATE COLLAR

The **BUCKLE COLLAR** is the standard collar used for everyday purposes. Be sure that you adjust the buckle on growing puppies. Check it every day. It can become too tight overnight! These collars can be made of leather or nylon. Attach your dog's identification tags to this collar.

The **CHOKE COLLAR** is designed for training, though it is not appropriate for the Crested Hairless or Powder Puff. It is constructed of highly polished steel so that it slides easily through the stainless steel loop. The idea is that the dog controls the pressure around its neck and he will stop pulling if the collar becomes uncomfortable. The choke collar is never left on a dog when not training.

The **HALTER** is for a trained dog that has to be restrained to prevent running away, chasing a cat and the like. Considered the most humane of all collars, it is frequently used on smaller dogs for which collars are not comfortable.

You can choose from an array of food and water bowls for your dog. Cresteds do not require large bowls, but they should be durable and safe.

PHOTO COURTESY OF MIKKI PET PRODUCTS.

find out what else you need as you go along—grooming supplies, flea/tick protection, baby gates to partition a room, etc. These things will vary depending on your situation, but it is important that you have everything you need to feed and make your Chinese Crested comfortable in his first few days at home.

PUPPY-PROOFING YOUR HOME

Aside from making sure that your Chinese Crested will be comfortable in your home, you also have to make sure that your home is safe for your Chinese Crested. This means taking precautions that your pup will not get into anything he should not get into and that there is nothing within his reach that may harm him should he sniff it, chew it, inspect it, etc. This probably seems obvious since, while you are primarily concerned with your pup's safety, at the same time you do not want your belongings to be ruined. Breakables should be placed out of reach if your dog is to have full run of the house. If he is to be limited to certain places within the house, keep any potentially dangerous items in the 'off-limits' areas.

An electrical cord can pose a danger should the puppy decide to taste it—and who is going to convince a pup that it would not make a great chew toy? Cords should be fastened tightly against

CHEMICAL TOXINS
Scour your garage for potential puppy dangers. Remove weed killers, pesticides and antifreeze materials. Antifreeze is highly toxic and even a few drops can kill an adult dog. The sweet taste attracts the animal, who will quickly consume it from the floor or curbside.

It is your responsibility to clean up after your dog has relieved himself. Pet shops sell various aids to assist in the clean-up task.

the wall. If your dog is going to spend time in a crate, make sure that there is nothing near his crate that he can reach if he sticks his curious little nose or paws through the openings. Just as you would with a child, keep all household cleaners and chemicals where the pup cannot reach them.

It is also important to make sure that the outside of your home is safe. Of course, your puppy should never be unsupervised, but a pup let loose in the garden will want to run and explore, and he should be granted that freedom.

A crate and your watchful eye are necessary for your pup's safety and to keep him from sticking his nose into trouble!

A safe chew toy will keep your pup occupied and his interests diverted from causing puppy mischief.

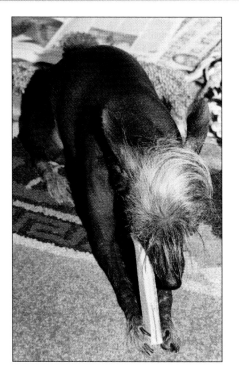

from digging underneath.

Be sure to repair or secure any gaps in the fence. Check the fence periodically to ensure that it is in good shape and make repairs as needed; a very determined pup may return to the same spot to 'work on it' until he is able to get through.

FIRST TRIP TO THE VET

You have selected your puppy, and your home and family are ready. Now all you have to do is collect your Chinese Crested from the breeder and the fun begins, right? Well…not so fast. Something else you need to plan is your pup's first trip to the veterinary surgeon. Perhaps the breeder can recommend someone in the area who is familiar with

Do not let a fence give you a false sense of security; you would be surprised at how crafty (and persistent) a dog can be in working out how to dig under and squeeze his way through small holes, or to jump or climb over a fence.

Chinese Cresteds can climb and dig, and they are definitely jumpers. Some think nothing of jumping on and off the dining room table, and they can spring like cats. For this reason, at least 6-foot-high fencing would be sensible, and make certain that the fence is well-embedded into the ground to prevent the dog

FINANCIAL RESPONSIBILITY

Grooming tools, collars, leashes, dog beds and, of course, toys will be an expense to you when you first obtain your pup, and the cost will continue throughout your dog's lifetime. If your puppy damages or destroys your possessions (as most puppies surely will!) or something belonging to a neighbour, you can calculate additional expense. There is also flea and pest control, which every dog owner faces more than once. You must be able to handle the financial responsibility of owning a dog.

schedule for the pup's vaccinations; the breeder will inform you of which ones the pup has already received and the vet can continue from there.

INTRODUCTION TO THE FAMILY

Everyone in the house will be excited about the puppy's coming home and will want to pet him and play with him, but it is best to make the introduction low-key

PUPPY-PROOFING

Thoroughly puppy-proof your house before bringing your puppy home. Never use cockroach or rodent poisons in any area accessible to the puppy. Avoid the use of toilet cleaners. Most dogs are born with 'toilet sonar' and will take a drink if the lid is left open. Also keep the rubbish secured and out of reach.

NATURAL TOXINS

Examine your grass and garden landscaping before bringing your puppy home. Many varieties of plants have leaves, stems or flowers that are toxic if ingested, and you can depend on a curious dog to investigate them. Ask your vet for information on poisonous plants or research them at your library.

Chinese Cresteds, or maybe you know some other Chinese Crested owners who can suggest a good vet. Either way, you should have an appointment arranged for your pup before you pick him up.

The pup's first visit will consist of an overall examination to make sure that the pup does not have any problems that are not apparent to you. The veterinary surgeon will also set up a

Your Crested's veterinary surgeon will soon become his OTHER best friend.

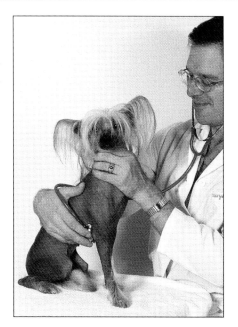

family members or may busy himself with exploring for a while. Gradually, each person should spend some time with the pup, one at a time, crouching down to get as close to the pup's level as possible, letting him sniff their hands and petting him gently. He definitely needs human attention and he needs to be touched—this is how to form an immediate bond. Just remember that the pup is experiencing many things for the first time, at the same time. There are new people, new noises, new smells and new things to investigate, so be gentle, be affectionate and be as comforting as you can be.

so as not to overwhelm the puppy. He is apprehensive already. It is the first time he has been separated from his mother and the breeder, and the ride to your home is likely to be the first time he has been in a car. The last thing you want to do is smother him, as this will only frighten him further. This is not to say that human contact is not extremely necessary at this stage, because this is the time when a connection between the pup and his human family is formed. Gentle petting and soothing words should help console him, as well as just putting him down and letting him explore on his own (under your watchful eye, of course).

The pup may approach the

A FORTNIGHT'S GRACE

It will take at least two weeks for your puppy to become accustomed to his new surroundings. Give him lots of love, attention, handling, frequent opportunities to relieve himself, a diet he likes to eat and a place he can call his own.

PUP'S FIRST NIGHT HOME

You have travelled home with your new charge safely in his crate. He's been to the vet for a thorough check-up; he's been weighed, his papers have been examined and perhaps he's even been vaccinated and wormed as well. He's met (and licked!) the whole family, including the excited children and the less-than-happy cat. He's explored his area, his new bed, the garden and anywhere else he's been permitted. He's eaten his first meal at home and relieved himself in the proper place. He's heard lots of new sounds, smelled new friends and seen more of the outside world than ever before...and that was just the first day! He's worn out and is ready for bed...or so you think!

It's puppy's first night home and you are ready to say 'Good night.' Keep in mind that this is his first night ever to be sleeping alone. His dam and littermates are no longer at paw's length and he's a bit scared, cold and lonely. Be reassuring to your new family member, but this is not the time to spoil him and give in to his inevitable whining.

Puppies whine. They whine to let others know where they are and hopefully to get company out of it. Place your pup in his new bed or crate in his designated area and close the door. Mercifully, he may fall asleep without a peep.

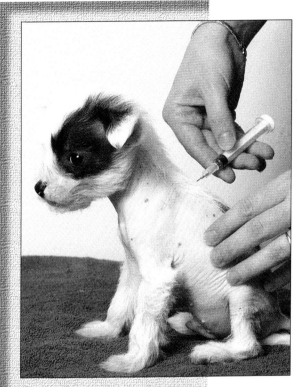

HOW VACCINES WORK

If you've just bought a puppy, you surely know the importance of having your pup vaccinated, but do you understand how vaccines work? Vaccines contain the same bacteria or viruses that cause the disease you want to prevent, but they have been chemically modified so that they don't cause any harm. Instead, the vaccine causes your dog to produce antibodies that fight the harmful bacteria. Thus, if your pup is exposed to the disease in the future, the antibodies will destroy the viruses or bacteria.

QUALITY FOOD
All dogs need a good-quality food with an adequate supply of protein to develop their bones and muscles properly. Most dogs are not picky eaters but, unless fed properly, can quickly succumb to skin problems.

When the inevitable occurs, however, ignore the whining—he is fine. Be strong and keep his interest in mind. Do not allow yourself to feel guilty and visit the pup. He will fall asleep eventually.

Many breeders recommend placing a piece of bedding from the pup's former home in his new crate so that he recognises and is comforted by the scent of his littermates. Others still advise placing a hot water bottle wrapped in a towel in the crate for warmth, which surely may remind him of mum or his missing siblings. As long as the pup doesn't attempt to suckle, this strategy may succeed!

Puppy's first night can be somewhat stressful for both the pup and his new family. Remember that you are setting the tone of night-time at your house. Unless you want to play with your pup every night at 10 p.m., midnight and 2 a.m., don't initiate the habit. Your family will thank you, and so will your pup!

PREVENTING PUPPY PROBLEMS

SOCIALISATION
Now that you have done all of the preparatory work and have helped your pup get accustomed to his new home and family, it is about time for you to have some

FEEDING TIPS
You will probably start feeding your pup the same food that he has been getting from the breeder; the breeder should give you a few days' supply to start you off. Although you should not give your pup too many treats, you will want to have puppy treats on hand for coaxing, training, rewards, etc. Be careful, though, as a small pup's calorie requirements are relatively low and a few treats can add up to almost a full day's worth of calories without the required nutrition.

fun! Socialising your Chinese Crested pup gives you the opportunity to show off your new friend, and your pup gets to reap the benefits of being an an exotic naked creature that people will want to meet and, in general, think is absolutely precious!

Besides getting to know his new family, your puppy should be exposed to other people, animals and situations. This will help him become well adjusted as he grows up and less prone to being timid or fearful of the new things he will encounter. Chinese Cresteds can tend to be shy, so socialisation is of utmost importance with this breed. Of course, your dog must not come into close contact with dogs you don't know well until his course of injections is fully complete.

Your pup's socialisation began with the breeder, but now it is your responsibility to continue it. The socialisation he receives until the age of 12 weeks is the most critical, as this is the time when he forms his impressions of the outside world. The eight-to-ten-week-old period is also known as the fear period. The interaction he receives during this time should be gentle and reassuring. Lack of socialisation, and/or negative experiences during the socialisation period, can manifest itself in fear and aggression as the dog grows up. Your puppy needs lots

THE RIDE HOME

Taking your dog from the breeder to your home in a car can be a very uncomfortable experience for both of you. The puppy will have been taken from his warm, friendly, safe environment and brought into a strange new environment—an environment that moves! Be prepared for loose bowels, urination, crying, whining and even fear biting. With proper love and encouragement when you arrive home, the stress of the trip should quickly disappear.

MEET THE WORLD
Thorough socialisation includes not only meeting new people but also being introduced to new experiences such as riding in the car, being groomed, hearing the television, walking in a crowd—the list is endless. The more your pup experiences, and the more positive the experiences are, the less of a shock and the less frightening it will be for your pup to encounter new things.

of positive interaction, which of course includes human contact, affection, handling and exposure to other animals. Some Chinese Cresteds will display aggression toward other dogs while some will not, but generally they will generally stand up for themselves, even against larger dogs. Socialisation will help to minimise any possibility of aggression.

Once your pup has received his necessary vaccinations, feel free to take him out and about (on his lead, of course). Walk him around the neighbourhood, take him on your daily errands, let people pet him, let him meet other dogs and pets, etc. Puppies do not have to try to make friends; there will be no shortage of people who will want to introduce themselves. Just make sure that you carefully supervise each meeting. If the neighbourhood children want to say hello, for example, that is great—children and pups most often make great companions. However, sometimes an excited child can unintentionally handle a pup too roughly, or an overzealous pup can playfully nip a little too hard. You want to make socialisation experiences positive ones. What a pup learns during this very formative stage will affect his attitude toward future encounters. You want your dog to be comfortable around everyone. A pup that has a bad experience with a child may grow up to be a dog that is shy around or aggressive toward children.

CONSISTENCY IN TRAINING
Dogs, being pack animals, naturally need a leader, or else they try to establish dominance in their packs. When you welcome a dog into your family, the choice of who becomes the leader and who

becomes the 'pack' is entirely up to you! Your pup's intuitive quest for dominance, coupled with the fact that it is nearly impossible to look at an irresistible Chinese Crested pup and not cave in, give the pup almost an unfair advantage in getting the upper hand! A pup will definitely test the waters to see what he can and cannot do. Do not give in to those

PROPER SOCIALISATION

The socialisation period for puppies is from age 8 to 16 weeks. This is the time when puppies need to leave their birth family and take up residence with their new owners, where they will meet many new people, other pets, etc. Failure to be adequately socialised can cause the dog to grow up fearing others and being shy and unfriendly due to a lack of self-confidence.

MANNERS MATTER

During the socialisation process, a puppy should meet people, experience different environments and definitely be exposed to other canines. Through playing and interacting with other dogs, your puppy will learn lessons, ranging from controlling the pressure of his jaws by biting his littermates to the inner-workings of the canine pack that he will apply to his human relationships for the rest of his life. That is why removing a puppy from its litter too early (before eight to ten weeks) can be detrimental to the pup's development.

pleading eyes—stand your ground when it comes to disciplining the pup and make sure that all family members do the same. It will only confuse the pup if Mother tells him to get off the sofa when he is used to sitting up there with Father to watch the nightly news. Avoid discrepancies by having all members of the household decide on the rules before the pup even comes home…and be consistent

Pups begin to learn the rules from adults in the pack. This Crested pup has an excellent teacher in a champion adult.

in enforcing them! Early training shapes the dog's personality, so you cannot be unclear in what you expect.

COMMON PUPPY PROBLEMS

The best way to prevent puppy problems is to be proactive in stopping an undesirable behaviour as soon as it starts. The old saying 'You can't teach an old dog new tricks' does not necessarily hold true, but it is true that it is much easier to discourage bad behaviour in a young developing pup than to wait until the pup's bad behaviour becomes the adult dog's bad habit. There are some problems that are especially prevalent in puppies as they develop.

NIPPING

As puppies start to teethe, they feel the need to sink their teeth into anything available... unfortunately, that usually includes your fingers, arms, hair and toes. You may find this behaviour cute for the first five seconds...until you feel just how sharp those puppy teeth are. Nipping is something you want to discourage immediately and consistently with a firm 'No!' (or whatever number of firm 'Nos' it takes for him to understand that you mean business). Then, replace your finger with an appropriate chew toy. While this behaviour is merely annoying when the dog is young, it can become dangerous as your Chinese Crested's adult teeth grow in and his jaws develop, and he continues to think it is okay to gnaw on human appendages. Your Chinese Crested does not mean any harm with a friendly nip, but he also does not know his own strength.

CRYING/WHINING

Your pup will often cry, whine, whimper, howl or make some type of commotion when he is left alone. This is basically his way of calling out for attention to make sure that you know he is there and that you have not forgotten about him. Your puppy feels insecure when he is left alone, when you are out of the house and he is in his crate or when you are in another part of the house and he cannot see you. The noise he is making is an expression of the anxiety he feels at being alone, so he needs to be taught that being alone is okay. You are not actually training the dog to stop making noise; rather, you are training him to feel comfortable when he is alone and thus removing the need for him to make the noise.

This is where the crate with cosy bedding and a toy comes in handy. You want to know that your pup is safe when you are not there to supervise, and you know that he will be safe in his crate

CHEWING TIPS
Chewing goes hand in hand with nipping in the sense that a teething puppy is always looking for a way to soothe his aching gums. In this case, instead of chewing on you, he may have taken a liking to your favourite shoe or something else which he should not be chewing. Again, realise that this is a normal canine behaviour that does not need to be discouraged, only redirected. Your pup just needs to be taught what is acceptable to chew on and what is off limits.

Consistently tell him NO when you catch him chewing on something forbidden and give him a chew toy. Conversely, praise him when you catch him chewing on something appropriate. In this way you are discouraging the inappropriate behaviour and reinforcing the desired behaviour. The puppy chewing should stop after his adult teeth have come in, but an adult dog continues to chew for various reasons—perhaps because he is bored, perhaps he needs to relieve tension or perhaps he just likes to chew. That is why it is important to redirect his chewing when he is still young.

PUPPY PROBLEMS

The majority of problems that are commonly seen in young pups will disappear as your dog gets older. However, how you deal with problems when he is young will determine how he reacts to discipline as an adult dog. It is important to establish who is boss (hopefully it will be you!) right away when you are first bonding with your dog. This bond will set the tone for the rest of your life together.

rather than roaming freely about the house. In order for the pup to stay in his crate without making a fuss, he first needs to be comfortable in his crate. On that note, it is extremely important that the crate is never used as a form of punishment; this will cause the pup to view the crate as a negative place, rather than as a place of his own for safety and retreat.

Accustom the pup to the crate in short, gradually increasing time intervals in which you put him in the crate, maybe with a treat, and stay in the room with him. If he cries or makes a fuss, do not go to him, but stay in his sight. Gradually he will realise that staying in his crate is all right without your help, and it will not be so traumatic for him when you are not around. You may want to leave the radio on softly when you leave the house; the sound of human voices may be comforting to him.

STRESS-FREE

Some experts in canine health advise that stress during a dog's early years of development can compromise and weaken his immune system, and may trigger the potential for a shortened life expectancy. They emphasise the need for happy and stress-free growing-up years.

A twelve-week-old pup, all settled in his new home.

FEEDING CONSIDERATIONS

A Chinese Crested Dog should be fed sensibly on a high-quality diet, but an owner should never be tempted to allow the dog to put on too much weight. An overweight Chinese Crested can not only look rather unsightly but also can suffer health problems as a result, as indeed can any overweight dog. Most owners like to feed two small meals each day, but however frequently you decide to feed your dog, remember that no dog should ever be fed within an hour of strenuous exercise.

There are now numerous high-quality canine foods available, and one of them is sure to suit your Chinese Crested. If you have chosen your breeder well, you should be able to obtain sound advice from that breeder as to which food they consider most suitable. When you buy your puppy, the breeder should provide you with a diet sheet giving details of exactly how your puppy has been fed. Of course, you will be at liberty to change that food as the youngster reaches adulthood, but this should be done gradually.

It is important that small dogs, if fed on proprietary foods, are given 'small bite' foods, for they will not be able to cope well with larger pieces. Some breeders also like to soak the food before

FEEDING TIP

You must store your dried dog food carefully. Open packages of dog food quickly lose their vitamin value, usually within 90 days of being opened. Mould spores and vermin could also contaminate the food.

feeding, especially if teeth are missing or loose.

Every breeder will have his or her own preference with regard to selection of food, but after the age of six months many select a lower protein diet than that which was given during the early months of life. Chicken-and-rice or lamb-and-rice diets seem to suit especially well. Chinese Crested Dogs that are susceptible to skin problems may find that if dairy products in the diet are kept to a bare minimum, it will help to alleviate the condition.

When selecting your dog's diet, three stages of development must be considered: the puppy stage, the adult stage and the senior or veteran stage.

PUPPY STAGE

Puppies instinctively want to suck milk from their mother's teats; a normal puppy will exhibit this behaviour just a few moments following birth. If puppies do not attempt to suckle within the first

FOOD PREFERENCE

Selecting the best dried dog food is difficult. There is no majority consensus among veterinary scientists as to the value of nutrient analyses (protein, fat, fibre, moisture, ash, cholesterol, minerals, etc.). All agree that feeding trials are what matter, but you also have to consider the individual dog. The dog's weight, age and activity level, and what pleases his taste, all must be considered. It is probably best to take the advice of your veterinary surgeon. Every dog's dietary requirements vary, even during the lifetime of a particular dog.

If your dog is fed a good dried food, it does not require supplements of meat or vegetables. Dogs do appreciate a little variety in their diets, so you may choose to stay with the same brand but vary the flavour. Alternatively, you may wish to add a little flavoured stock to give a difference to the taste.

TEST FOR PROPER DIET

A good test for proper diet is the colour, odour and firmness of your dog's stool. A healthy dog usually produces three semi-hard stools per day. The stools should have no unpleasant odour. They should be the same colour from excretion to excretion.

Pups are given milk meals as part of the weaning process.

nurse from their mothers for about the first six weeks, although, starting around the third or fourth week, the breeder will begin to introduce small portions of suitable solid food. Most breeders like to introduce alternate milk and meat meals initially, building up to weaning time.

By the time the puppies are seven or a maximum of eight weeks old, they should be fully weaned and fed solely on a proprietary puppy food. Selection of the most suitable, good-quality diet at this time is essential, for a puppy's fastest growth rate is during the first year of life. Veterinary surgeons are usually able to offer advice in this regard, but Chinese Cresteds are usually switched to adult food at around six months of age, depending on

half-hour or so, they should be encouraged to do so by placing them on the nipples, having selected ones with plenty of milk. This early milk supply is important in providing the essential colostrum, which protects the puppies during the first eight to ten weeks of their lives. Although a mother's milk is much better than any milk formula, despite there being some excellent ones available, if the puppies do not feed, the breeder will have to feed them by hand. For those with less experience, advice from a veterinary surgeon is important so that not only the right quantity of milk is fed but also that of correct quality, fed at suitably frequent intervals, usually every two hours during the first few days of life.

Puppies should be allowed to

CHANGE IN DIET

As your dog's caretaker, you know the importance of keeping his diet consistent, but sometimes when you run out of food or if you're on holiday, you have to make a change quickly. Some dogs will experience digestive problems, but most will not. If you are planning on changing your dog's menu, do so gradually to ensure that your dog will not have any problems. Over a period of four to five days, slowly add some new food to your dog's old food, increasing the percentage of new food each day.

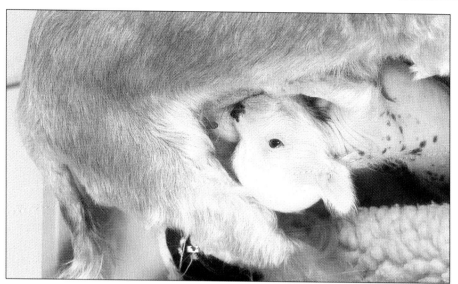

Puppies should be allowed to nurse from their mothers for the first six weeks and should be fully weaned by eight weeks of age.

what they have been fed. Again, it is important that they are fed 'small-bite' food, as they will not be able to cope with large pieces. Puppy and junior diets should be well balanced for the needs of your dog so that, except in certain circumstances, additional vitamins, minerals and proteins will not be required.

ADULT DIETS

A dog is considered an adult when it has stopped growing. Chinese Cresteds generally reach full height at around nine months of age, but are often switched to an adult diet at about six months of age. Again you should rely upon your veterinary surgeon or dietary specialist to recommend an acceptable maintenance diet. Major dog food manufacturers

specialise in this type of food, and it is merely necessary for you to select the one best suited to your dog's needs. Active dogs may have different requirements than sedate dogs.

VETERAN DIETS

As dogs get older, their metabolism changes. The older dog usually exercises less, moves more slowly and sleeps more. This change in lifestyle and physiological performance requires a change in diet. Since these changes take place slowly, they might not be recognisable. What is easily recognisable is weight gain. By continuing to feed your dog an adult-maintenance diet when it is slowing down metabolically, your dog will gain weight. Obesity in an older dog

What are you feeding your dog?

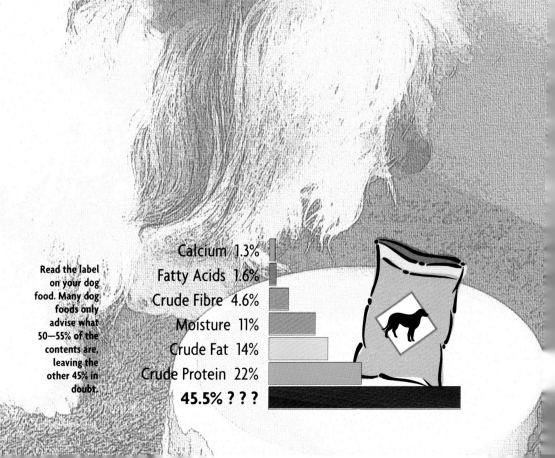

Read the label on your dog food. Many dog foods only advise what 50—55% of the contents are, leaving the other 45% in doubt.

Calcium 1.3%
Fatty Acids 1.6%
Crude Fibre 4.6%
Moisture 11%
Crude Fat 14%
Crude Protein 22%
45.5% ? ? ?

compounds the health problems that already accompany old age.

As your dog gets older, few of his organs function up to par. The kidneys slow down and the intestines become less efficient. These age-related factors are best handled with a change in diet and a change in feeding schedule to give smaller portions that are more easily digested. There is no single best diet for every older dog. While many dogs do well on light or

GRAIN-BASED DIETS

Some less expensive dog foods are based on grains and other plant proteins. While these products may appear to be attractively priced, many breeders prefer a diet based on animal proteins and believe that they are more conducive to your dog's health. Many grain-based diets rely on soy protein, which may cause flatulence (passing gas).

There are many cases, however, when your dog might require a special diet. These special requirements should only be recommended by your veterinary surgeon.

DRINK, DRANK, DRUNK— MAKE IT A DOUBLE

In both humans and dogs, as well as most living organisms, water forms the major part of nearly every body tissue. Naturally, we take water for granted, but without it, life as we know it would cease.

For dogs, water is needed to keep their bodies functioning biochemically. Additionally, water is needed to replace the water lost while panting to cool down (or, in the unique case of the Chinese Crested, while sweating to cool down). Humans lose electrolyte-containing products and other body-fluid components through sweating; dogs do not lose anything except water.

Water is essential always, but especially so when the weather is hot or humid or when your dog is exercising or working vigorously.

senior diets, other dogs do better on puppy diets or other special premium diets such as lamb and rice. Be sensitive to your senior Chinese Crested's diet, as this will help control other problems that may arise with your old friend.

WATER

Just as your dog needs proper nutrition from his food, water is an essential 'nutrient' as well. Water keeps the dog's body properly hydrated and promotes normal function of the body's systems. During house-training it is necessary to keep an eye on how much water your Chinese Crested is drinking, but once he is reliably trained he should have

TIPPING THE SCALES

Good nutrition is vital to your dog's health, but many people end up over-feeding or giving unnecessary supplements. Here are some common doggie diet don'ts:

- Adding milk, yoghurt and cheese to your dog's diet may seem like a good idea for coat and skin care, but dairy products can be the cause of skin problems in Cresteds, are very fattening and can cause indigestion.
- Diets high in fat will not cause heart attacks in dogs but will certainly cause your dog to gain weight.
- Most importantly, don't assume your dog will simply stop eating once he doesn't need any more food. Given the chance, he will eat you out of house and home!

stand its ground against other dogs, and a meeting with a large aggressive dog may not be a happy one!

Keep in mind, too, that Chinese Crested Dogs in general are very proficient jumpers. In consequence, when given freedom off the lead, in the garden or even around the home, they are capable of jumping higher walls and fences than might be expected.

Not all Chinese Crested owners live in houses with gardens, but those that do often

'DOES THIS COLLAR MAKE ME LOOK FAT?'

While humans may obsess about how they look and how trim their bodies are, many people believe that extra weight on their dogs is a good thing. The truth is, pets should not be over- or under-weight, as both can lead to or signal sickness. In order to tell how fit your pet is, run your hands over his ribs. Are his ribs buried under a layer of fat or are they sticking out considerably? If your pet is within his normal weight range, you should be able to feel the ribs easily, but they should not protrude abnormally. If you stand above him, the outline of his body should resemble an hourglass. Some breeds do tend to be leaner while some are a bit stockier, but making sure your dog is the right weight for his breed will certainly contribute to his good health.

access to clean fresh water at all times, especially if you feed dried food. Make certain that the dog's water bowl is clean, and change the water often.

EXERCISE

Chinese Crested Dogs, although small, are active; they require and thoroughly enjoy exercise. They will usually be more than happy to be taken for on-lead walks, and will also enjoy free run, though owners should be careful that the areas in which their dogs exercise are thoroughly safe. Keep in mind that a Chinese Crested is likely to find that their dogs exercise themselves quite happily on their own grounds, especially if more than one dog is kept in the family. For those owners living in flats, regular on-lead walks are necessary.

To keep any breed of dog healthy, it is essential that opportunity be given to build up muscle tone. This important part of canine care should never be overlooked, even in a breed as

FEEDING TIPS

Dog food must be at room temperature, neither too hot nor too cold. Fresh water, changed daily and served in a clean bowl, is mandatory, especially when feeding dried food.

Never feed your dog from the table while you are eating, and never feed your dog leftovers from your own meal. They usually contain too much fat and too much seasoning.

Dogs must chew their food. Hard pellets are excellent; soups and slurries are to be avoided.

Don't add leftovers or any extras to normal dog food. The normal food is usually balanced, and adding something extra destroys the balance.

Except for age-related changes, dogs do not require dietary variations. They can be fed the same diet, day after day, without becoming ill.

DO DOGS HAVE TASTE BUDS?

Watching a dog 'wolf' or gobble his food, seemingly without chewing, leads an owner to wonder whether their dogs can taste anything. Yes, dogs have taste buds, with sensory perception of sweet, salty and sour. Puppies are born with fully mature taste buds.

small as the Chinese Crested. Likewise, bear in mind that an overweight dog should never be suddenly over-exercised; instead he should be encouraged to increase exercise slowly. Not only is exercise essential to keep the dog's body fit, it is essential to his mental well-being. A bored dog will find something to do, which often manifests itself in some type of destructive behaviour. In this sense, exercise is essential for the owner's mental well-being as well!

Grooming tools are available at your local pet shop, where you can select what you need for maintaining your Crested's skin and coat.

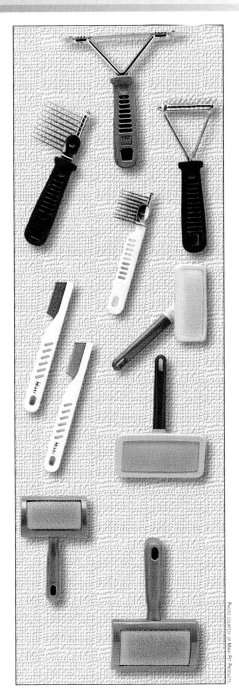

PHOTO COURTESY OF MIKKI PET PRODUCTS.

GROOMING

BASIC MAINTENANCE

There is rather more in the way of coat maintenance for a Powder Puff than for a Hairless Chinese Crested, but both will need to be bathed fairly frequently to keep skin and coat in good condition. It must be stressed that although it is always important to rinse thoroughly after shampooing, this is especially so in the case of the Hairless variety.

Some owners of hairless dogs like to rub them down with glycerine immediately following a bath to prevent the skin from becoming too dry. It is also wise to apply a suitable cream on the body quite frequently to maintain

GROOMING EQUIPMENT

How much grooming equipment you purchase will depend on how much grooming you are going to do. Here are some basics:
- Natural bristle brush
- Skin cream (Hairless)
- Metal comb
- Scissors
- Blaster
- Rubber mat
- Dog shampoo
- Spray hose attachment
- Ear cleaner
- Cotton wipes
- Towels
- Nail clippers

the skin's suppleness. The skin quality on Chinese Crested Dogs varies, so each owner will undoubtedly find the type of moisturising agent that best suits his or her own dog.

Some Hairless Chinese Crested Dogs grow hair in places where it is not desirable. If this is the case, unwanted areas of hair growth are often carefully and discreetly removed. The method of removal is very much a matter of personal preference, but some owners like to use a moustache/beard trimmer, which is both inexpensive and relatively quiet.

In a Powder Puff, any mats or tangles in the coat must always be carefully removed prior to bathing. Although the Powder Puff is long coated, this is by no means a difficult coat to maintain; a thorough weekly brush and comb will usually be sufficient for good condition.

The plumes of hair on head, ears, feet and tail of a Hairless should be carefully groomed through regularly. This will avoid any mats forming and enable the plumage to hang freely.

BATHING

Dogs do not need to be bathed as often as humans, but regular bathing of the Chinese Crested is essential for healthy skin and/or a healthy, shiny coat. Again, like most anything, if you accustom your pup to being bathed as a

SOAP IT UP

The use of human soap products like shampoo, bubble bath and hand soap can be damaging to a dog's coat and skin. Human products are too strong; they remove the protective oils coating the dog's hair and skin that make him water-resistant. Use only shampoo made especially for dogs. You may like to use a medicated shampoo, which will help to keep external parasites at bay.

puppy, it will be second nature by the time he grows up. You want your dog to be at ease in the bath or else it could end up a wet, soapy, messy ordeal for both of you!

(Above) The plumes (head, feet, tail) on the Hairless should be brushed through regularly to prevent mats and to encourage the fringe to fall freely. (Below) The Powder Puff's coat, though long, is easy to maintain with regular brushing and combing.

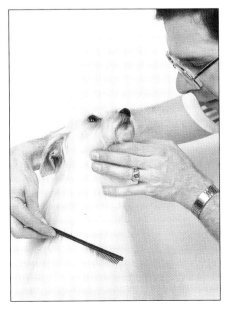

With the Powder Puff, brush him thoroughly before wetting his coat. This will get rid of most mats and tangles, which are harder to remove when the coat is wet. Make certain that your dog has a good non-slip surface on which to stand. Begin by wetting the dog's skin or coat, checking the water temperature to make sure that it is neither too hot nor too cold. A shower or hose attachment is necessary for thoroughly wetting and rinsing the dog.

Next, apply shampoo and work it into a good lather. Wash the head last, as you do not want shampoo to drip into the dog's eyes while you are washing the rest of his body. You should use only a shampoo that is made for dogs. Do not use a product made for humans. You can use this opportunity to check the skin for any bumps, bites or other abnormalities. Do not neglect any area of the body—get all of the hard-to-reach places.

Once the dog has been thoroughly shampooed, he requires an equally thorough rinsing. Shampoo left on the skin or in the coat can be irritating to the dog's skin. Protect his eyes from the shampoo by shielding them with your hand and directing the flow of water in the opposite direction. You should also avoid getting water in the ear canal.

EAR CLEANING

The ears should be kept clean with a cotton wipe and ear powder made especially for dogs; do not probe into the ear canal with a cotton bud, as this can cause injury. Be on the lookout for any signs of infection or ear mite infestation. If your Chinese Crested has been shaking his head or scratching at his ears frequently, this usually indicates a problem. If the dog's ears have an unusual odour, this is a sure sign of mite infestation or infection, and a signal to have his ears checked by the veterinary surgeon.

TOENAIL MAINTENANCE

Care should always be taken that toenails are in good condition and not causing any discomfort, but the Chinese Crested's nails are usually kept somewhat longer than those of other breeds, in accordance with the breed standard. Before trimming your Crested's nails, consult a breeder or groomer to learn the proper length at which you should maintain them.

Your Chinese Crested should be accustomed to having his nails trimmed at an early age, as it will be part of your grooming mainte- nance routine. Before you start cutting, make sure you can identify the 'quick' in each nail. The quick is a blood vessel that runs through the centre of each

(Above) Cream is applied to the Hairless's skin, both after bathing to prevent dryness and before an appear- ance in the show ring to give the skin a smooth, supple look. (Below) Cleaning these ears is serious business! It is not advised to probe into the ear with a cotton bud, as shown here, but rather to use a soft wipe and ear cleaner made for dogs.

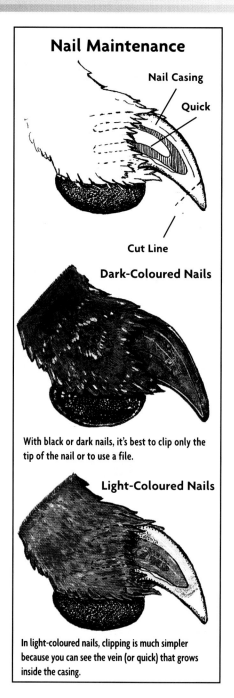

Nail Maintenance

Nail Casing

Quick

Cut Line

Dark-Coloured Nails

With black or dark nails, it's best to clip only the tip of the nail or to use a file.

Light-Coloured Nails

In light-coloured nails, clipping is much simpler because you can see the vein (or quick) that grows inside the casing.

PEDICURE TIP

A dog that spends a lot of time outside on a hard surface, such as cement or pavement, will have his nails naturally worn down and may not need to have them trimmed as often, except maybe in the colder months when he is not outside as much. Regardless, it is best to get your dog accustomed to the nail-trimming procedure at an early age so that he is used to it. Some dogs are especially sensitive about having their feet touched, but if a dog has experienced it since puppyhood, it should not bother him.

nail and grows rather close to the end. The quick will bleed if accidentally cut, which will be quite painful for the dog as it contains nerve endings. Keep some type of clotting agent on hand, such as a styptic pencil or styptic powder (the type used for shaving). This will stop the bleeding quickly when applied to the end of the cut nail. Do not panic if you cut the quick, just stop the bleeding and talk soothingly to your dog. Once he has calmed down, move on to the next nail. It is better to clip a little at a time, particularly with black-nailed dogs.

Hold your pup steady as you begin trimming his nails; you do not want him to make any sudden movements or run away. Talk to him soothingly and stroke him as you clip. Holding his foot in your hand, simply take off the end of each nail with one swift clip. You should purchase nail clippers that are made for use on dogs; you can find them wherever you buy pet or grooming supplies.

TEETH

Teeth should always be kept as free from tartar as possible. There are now several canine tooth-cleaning agents available, including small toothbrushes and canine toothpaste.

TRAVELLING WITH YOUR DOG

CAR TRAVEL

You should accustom your Chinese Crested to riding in a car at an early age. You may or may not take him in the car often, but at the very least he will need to go to the vet and you do not want these trips to be traumatic for the dog or troublesome for you. The safest way for a dog to ride in the car is in his crate. If he uses a crate in the house, you can use the same crate for travel.

Put the pup in the crate and see how he reacts. If he seems uneasy, you can have a passenger hold him on his lap while you drive. Another option for car travel is a specially made safety harness for dogs, which straps the dog in much like a seat belt. Do not let the dog roam loose in the vehicle—this is very dangerous! If you should stop short, your dog can be thrown and injured. If the dog starts climbing on you and pestering you while you are driving, you will not be able to concentrate on the road. It is an unsafe situation for everyone—human and canine.

DEADLY DECAY
Did you know that periodontal disease (a condition of the bone and gums surrounding a tooth) can be fatal? Having your dog's teeth and mouth checked regularly can prevent it.

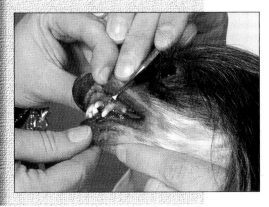

For long trips, be prepared to stop to let the dog relieve himself. Take with you whatever you need to clean up after him, including some paper kitchen towels and perhaps some old towelling for use should he have a toileting accident in the car or suffer from travel sickness.

AIR TRAVEL

While it is possible to take a dog on a flight within Britain, this is fairly unusual and advance permission is always required. The dog will be required to travel in a fibreglass crate and you should always check in advance with the airline regarding specific requirements. To help put the dog at ease, give him one of his favourite toys in the crate. Do not feed the dog for at least six hours before the trip in order to minimise his need to relieve himself. However, certain regulations specify that water must always be made available to the dog in the crate.

Make sure your dog is properly identified and that your contact information appears on his ID tags and on his crate. Animals travel in a different area of the plane than human passengers, so every rule must be strictly followed so as to prevent the risk of getting separated from your dog.

HOMESITTING

Another option for the travelling dog owner is the homesitter. These unique organisations are comprised of bonded individuals who will stay at your home to look after your pet and property while you are away. Currently these homesitters can be found throughout the UK and are a most convenient option. If the sitter is bonded, owners may receive a reduced insurance premium benefit.

LET THE SUN SHINE

Your dog needs daily sunshine for the same reason people do. Pets kept inside homes with curtains drawn against the sun suffer from 'SAD' (Seasonal Affected Disorder) to the same degree as humans. We now know that sunlight must enter the iris and thus progress to the pineal gland to regulate the body's hormonal system. When we live and work in artificial light, both circadian rhythms and hormone balances are disturbed.

Take care of your Hairless' delicate skin in the sun; some owners like to use a cream that contains sunscreen.

BOARDING

So you want to take a family holiday—and you want to include *all* members of the family. You would probably make arrangements for accommodation ahead of time anyway, but this is especially important when travelling with a dog. You do not want to make an overnight stop at the only place around for miles, only to find out that they do not allow dogs. Also, you do not want to reserve a place for your family without confirming that you are travelling with a dog, because, if it is against their policy, you may end up without a place to stay.

Alternatively, if you are travelling and choose not to bring your Chinese Crested, you will have to make arrangements for him while you are away. Some options are to take him to a neighbour's house to stay while you are gone, to have a trusted neighbour pop in often or stay at your house or to bring your dog to a reputable boarding kennel. If you choose to board him at a kennel, you should visit in advance to see the facilities provided and where the dogs are kept. Are the dogs' areas spacious and kept clean? Talk to some of the employees and see how they treat the dogs—do they spend time with the dogs, play with them, exercise them, etc.? Are they knowledgeable about the Chinese Crested?

Also find out the kennel's policy on vaccinations and what they require. This is for all of the dogs' safety, since there is a greater risk of diseases being

Locate and research boarding kennels in your area, and have a kennel selected before you actually need to use it. This way, you will be confident about leaving your dog in the kennel's care.

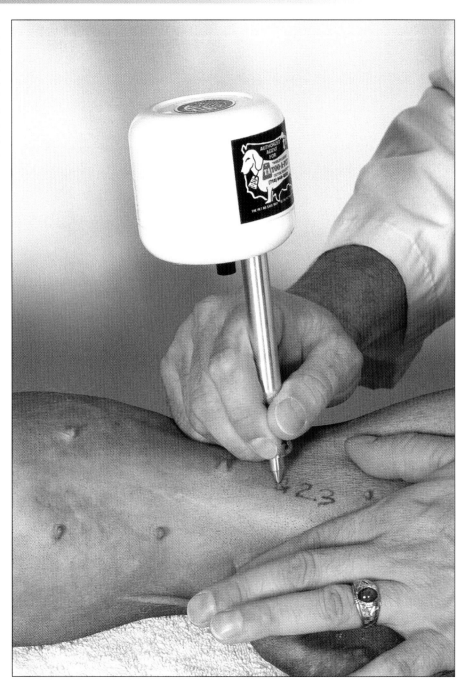

Chinese Crested being tattooed by the veterinary surgeon. Tattooing is a more permanent form of identification than the more common collar and ID tag.

passed from dog to dog when dogs are kept together.

IDENTIFICATION

Your Chinese Crested is your valued companion and friend. That is why you always keep a close eye on him and you have made sure that he cannot escape from the garden or wriggle out of his collar and run away from you. However, accidents can happen and there may come a time when your dog unexpectedly becomes separated from you. If this unfortunate event should occur, the first thing on your mind will be finding him. Proper identification, including an ID tag, a tattoo and possibly a microchip, will increase the chances of his being returned to you safely and quickly.

IDENTIFICATION OPTIONS

As puppies become more and more expensive, especially those puppies of high quality for showing and/or breeding, they have a greater chance of being stolen. The usual collar dog tag is, of course, easily removed. But there are two more permanent techniques that have become widely used for identification.

The puppy microchip implantation involves the injection of a small microchip, about the size of a corn kernel, under the skin of the dog. If your dog shows up at a clinic or shelter, or is offered for resale under less than savoury circumstances, it can be positively identified by the microchip. The microchip is scanned, and a registry quickly identifies you as the owner. This is not only protection against theft, but should the dog run away or go chasing a squirrel and become lost, you have a fair chance of his being returned to you.

Tattooing is done on various parts of the dog, from his belly to his cheeks. The number tattooed can be your telephone number or any other number that you can easily memorise. When professional dog thieves see a tattooed dog, they usually lose interest. Both microchipping and tattooing can be done at your local veterinary clinic. For the safety of our dogs, no laboratory facility or dog broker will accept a tattooed dog as stock.

A suitable dog tag will assist someone who finds a lost dog in reuniting the dog with his owners.

Living with an untrained dog is a lot like owning a piano that you do not know how to play—it is a nice object to look at but it does not do much more than that to bring you pleasure. Now try taking piano lessons, and suddenly the piano comes alive and brings forth magical sounds and rhythms that set your heart singing and your body swaying.

The same is true with your Chinese Crested. Any dog is a big responsibility and, if not trained sensibly, may develop unacceptable behaviour that annoys you or could even cause family friction.

To train your Chinese Crested, you may like to enrol in an obedience class. Teach your dog good manners as you learn how and why he behaves the way he does. Find out how to communicate with your dog and how to recognise and understand his communications with you.

A well-trained Chinese Crested embodies grace, intelligence and good behaviour, and will be a wonderful companion with whom to share your home.

Suddenly the dog takes on a new role in your life—he is clever, interesting, well behaved and fun to be with. He demonstrates his bond of devotion to you daily. In other words, your Chinese Crested does wonders for your ego because he constantly reminds you that you are not only his leader, you are his hero!

Those involved with teaching dog obedience and counselling owners about their dogs' behaviour have discovered some interesting facts about dog ownership. For example, training dogs when they are puppies results in the highest rate of success in developing well-mannered and well-adjusted adult dogs. Training an older dog, from six months to six years of age, can produce almost equal results providing that the owner accepts the dog's slower rate of learning capability and is willing to work patiently to help the dog succeed at developing to his fullest potential. Unfortunately, many owners of untrained adult dogs lack the patience factor, so they do not persist until their dogs are successful at learning particular behaviours.

Training a puppy aged 10 to 16 weeks (20 weeks at the most) is like working with a dry sponge in a pool of water. The pup soaks up whatever you show him and constantly looks for more things to do and learn. At this early age,

PARENTAL GUIDANCE

Training a dog is a life experience. Many parents admit that much of what they know about raising children they learned from caring for their dogs. Dogs respond to love, fairness and guidance, just as children do. Become a good dog owner and you may become an even better parent.

his body is not yet producing hormones, and therein lies the reason for such a high rate of success. Without hormones, he is focused on his owners and not particularly interested in investigating other places, dogs, people,

MEALTIME

Mealtime should be a peaceful time for your Chinese Crested. Do not put his food and water bowls in a high-traffic area in the house. For example, give him his own little corner of the kitchen where he can eat undisturbed and where he will not be underfoot. Do not allow small children or other family members to disturb the dog when he is eating.

THINK BEFORE YOU BARK

Dogs are sensitive to their masters' moods and emotions. Use your voice wisely when communicating with your dog. Never raise your voice at your dog unless you are angry and trying to correct him. 'Barking' at your dog can become as meaningless as 'dogspeak' is to you. Think before you bark!

etc. You are his leader: his provider of food, water, shelter and security. He latches onto you and wants to stay close. He will usually follow you from room to room, will not let you out of his sight when you are outdoors with him and will respond in like manner to the people and animals you encounter. If you greet a friend warmly, he will be happy to greet the person as well. If, however, you are hesitant or anxious about the approach of a stranger, he will respond accordingly.

Once the puppy begins to produce hormones, his natural curiosity emerges and he begins to investigate the world around him. It is at this time when you may notice that the untrained dog begins to wander away from you and even ignore your commands to stay close. When this behaviour becomes a problem, you have two choices: get rid of the dog or train

THE HAND THAT FEEDS

To a dog's way of thinking, your hands are like his mouth in terms of a defence mechanism. If you squeeze him too tightly, he might just bite you because that would be his normal response. This is not aggressive biting and, although all biting should be discouraged, you need the discipline in learning how to handle your dog.

HONOUR AND OBEY

Dogs are the most honourable animals in existence. They consider another species (humans) as their own. They interface with you. You are their leader. Puppies perceive children to be on their level; their actions around small children are different from their behaviour around their adult masters.

him. It is strongly urged that you choose the latter option.

You usually will be able to find obedience classes within a reasonable distance from your home, but you can also do a lot to train your dog yourself. Sometimes there are classes available, but the tuition is too costly. Whatever the circumstances, the solution to training your dog without obedience classes lies within the pages of this book.

This chapter is devoted to helping you train your Chinese Crested at home. If the recommended procedures are followed faithfully, you may expect positive results that will prove rewarding both to you and your dog.

Whether your new charge is a puppy or a mature adult, the methods of teaching and the techniques we use in training basic behaviours are the same. After all, no dog, whether puppy or adult, likes harsh or inhumane methods. All creatures, however, respond favourably to gentle motivational methods and sincere praise and encouragement. Now let us get started.

TOILET TRAINING

You can train a puppy to relieve himself wherever you choose, but this must be somewhere suitable. You should bear in mind from the outset that when your puppy is old enough to go out in public places, any canine deposits must be removed at once. You will always have to carry with you a small plastic bag or 'poop-scoop.'

Outdoor training includes such surfaces as grass, gravel and cement. Indoor training usually

TRAINING TIP

Dogs will do anything for your attention. If you reward the dog when he is calm and resting, you will develop a well-mannered dog. If, on the other hand, you greet your dog excitedly and encourage him to wrestle with you, the dog will greet you the same way and you will have a hyperactive dog on your hands.

REAP THE REWARDS

If you start with a normal, healthy dog and give him time, patience and some carefully executed lessons, you will reap the rewards of that training for the life of the dog. And what a life it will be! The two of you will find immeasurable pleasure in the companionship you have built together with love, respect and understanding.

means training your dog to newspaper. When deciding on the surface and location that you will want your Chinese Crested to use, be sure it is going to be permanent. Training your dog to grass and then changing your mind a few months later is extremely difficult for both dog and owner.

Next, choose the command you will use each and every time you want your puppy to void. 'Hurry up' and 'Toilet' are examples of commands commonly used by dog owners. Get in the habit of giving the

CANINE DEVELOPMENT SCHEDULE

It is important to understand how and at what age a puppy develops into adulthood. If you are a puppy owner, consult the following Canine Development Schedule to determine the stage of development your puppy is currently experiencing. This knowledge will help you as you work with the puppy in the weeks and months ahead.

Period	Age	Characteristics
FIRST TO THIRD	BIRTH TO SEVEN WEEKS	Puppy needs food, sleep and warmth, and responds to simple and gentle touching. Needs mother for security and disciplining. Needs littermates for learning and interacting with other dogs. Pup learns to function within a pack and learns pack order of dominance. Begin socialising with adults and children for short periods. Begins to become aware of its environment.
FOURTH	EIGHT TO TWELVE WEEKS	Brain is fully developed. Needs socialising with outside world. Remove from mother and littermates. Needs to change from canine pack to human pack. Human dominance necessary. Fear period occurs between 8 and 12 weeks. Avoid fright and pain.
FIFTH	THIRTEEN TO SIXTEEN WEEKS	Training and formal obedience should begin. Less association with other dogs, more with people, places, situations. Period will pass easily if you remember this is pup's change-to-adolescence time. Be firm and fair. Flight instinct prominent. Permissiveness and over-disciplining can do permanent damage. Praise for good behaviour.
JUVENILE	FOUR TO EIGHT MONTHS	Another fear period about 7 to 8 months of age. It passes quickly, but be cautious of fright and pain. Sexual maturity reached. Dominant traits established. Dog should understand sit, down, come and stay by now.

NOTE: THESE ARE APPROXIMATE TIME FRAMES. ALLOW FOR INDIVIDUAL DIFFERENCES IN PUPPIES.

puppy your chosen relief command before you take him out. That way, when he becomes an adult, you will be able to determine if he wants to go out when you ask him. A confirmation will be signs of interest, wagging his tail, watching you intently, going to the door, etc.

PAPER CAPER

Never line your pup's sleeping area with newspaper. Puppy litters are usually raised on newspaper and, once in your home, the puppy will immediately associate newspaper with voiding. Never put newspaper on any floor while house-training, as this will only confuse the puppy. If you are paper-training him, use paper in his designated relief area ONLY. Finally, restrict water intake after evening meals. Offer a few licks at a time—never let a young puppy gulp water after meals.

THE GOLDEN RULE

The golden rule of dog training is simple. For each 'question' (command), there is only one correct answer (reaction). One command = one reaction. Keep practising the command until the dog reacts correctly without hesitating. Be repetitive but not monotonous. Dogs get bored just as people do!

PUPPY'S NEEDS

Puppy needs to relieve himself after play periods, after each meal, after he has been sleeping and at any time he indicates that he is looking for a place to urinate or defecate. The urinary and intestinal tract muscles of very young puppies are not fully developed. Therefore, like human babies, puppies need to relieve themselves frequently.

Take your puppy out often— every hour for an eight-week-old, for example—-and always immediately after sleeping and eating. The older the puppy, the less often he will need to relieve himself. Finally, as a mature healthy adult, he will require only three to five relief trips per day.

HOUSING

Since the types of housing and control you provide for your puppy have a direct relationship on the success of house-training, we consider the various aspects of both before we begin training.

Taking a new puppy home and turning him loose in your house can be compared to turning a child loose in a sports arena and telling the child that the place is all his! The sheer enormity of the place would be too much for him to handle. Instead, offer the puppy clearly defined areas where he can play, sleep, eat and live. A room of the house where the family gathers is the most obvious choice. Puppies are social animals and need to feel a part of the pack right from the start. Hearing your voice, watching you while you are doing things and smelling you nearby are all positive reinforcers that he is now a member of your pack. Usually a family room, the kitchen or a nearby adjoining breakfast area is ideal for providing safety and security for both puppy and owner.

Within the designated room, there should be a smaller area that the puppy can call his own. An

COMMAND STANCE
Stand up straight and authoritatively when giving your dog commands. Do not issue commands when lying on the floor or lying on your back on the sofa. If you are on your hands and knees when you give a command, your dog will think you are positioning yourself to play.

TAKE THE LEAD
Do not carry your dog to his toilet area. Lead him there on a leash or, better yet, encourage him to follow you to the spot. If you start carrying him to his spot, you might end up doing this routine forever and your dog will have the satisfaction of having trained YOU.

alcove, a wire or fibreglass dog crate or a fenced (not boarded!) corner from which he can view the activities of his new family will be fine. The size of the area or crate is the key factor here. The area must be large enough so that the puppy can lie down and stretch out, as well as stand up, without rubbing his head on the top. At the same time, it must be small enough so that he cannot relieve himself at one end and sleep at the other without coming into contact with his droppings until fully trained to relieve himself outside. Dogs are, by nature, clean animals and will not remain close to their relief areas unless forced to do so. In those cases, they then become dirty dogs and usually remain that way for life.

The dog's designated area should contain clean bedding and a toy. Water must always be available, in a non-spill container.

Nothing gets a pup's attention more quickly than a tasty titbit! Treats can be very helpful motivators in teaching new commands.

ATTENTION!
Your dog is actually training you at the same time you are training him. Dogs do things to get attention. They usually repeat whatever succeeds in getting your attention.

CONTROL

By control, we mean helping the puppy to create a lifestyle pattern that will be compatible to that of his human pack (YOU!). Just as we guide little children to learn our way of life, we must show the puppy when it is time to play, eat, sleep, exercise and even entertain himself.

Your puppy should always sleep in his crate. He should also learn that, during times of household confusion and excessive human activity, such as at breakfast when family members are preparing for the day, he can play by himself in relative safety and comfort in his designated area. Each time you leave the puppy alone, he should understand exactly where he is to stay.

Puppies are chewers. They cannot tell the difference between lamp cords, television wires, shoes, table legs, etc. Chewing into a television wire, for example, can be fatal to the puppy, while a shorted wire can start a fire in the house. If the puppy chews on the arm of the chair when he is alone, you will probably discipline him angrily when you get home. Thus, he makes the association that your coming home means he is going to be punished. (He will not remember chewing the chair and is incapable of making the association of the discipline with his naughty deed.) Accustoming the pup to his designated area not only keeps him safe but also avoids his engaging in destructive behaviours when you are not around.

Times of excitement, such as special occasions, family parties, etc., can be fun for the puppy providing that he can view the activities from the security of his designated area. He is not underfoot and he is not being fed all sorts of titbits that will probably cause him stomach distress, yet he still feels a part of the fun.

SCHEDULE

A puppy should be taken to his relief area each time he is released from his designated area, after meals, after a play session and when he first awakens in the morning (at age eight weeks, this can mean 5 a.m.!). The puppy will indicate that he's ready 'to go' by circling or sniffing busily—do not misinterpret these signs. For a puppy less than ten weeks of age, a routine of taking him out every

PRACTICE MAKES PERFECT!

• Have training lessons with your dog every day in several short segments—three to five times a day for a few minutes at a time is ideal.
• Do not have long practice sessions. The dog will become easily bored.
• Never practise when you are tired, ill, worried or in an otherwise negative mood. This will transmit to the dog and may have an adverse effect on its performance.

Think fun, short and above all POSITIVE! End each session on a high note, rather than a failed exercise, and make sure to give a lot of praise. Enjoy the training and help your dog enjoy it, too.

hour is necessary. As the puppy grows, he will be able to wait for longer periods of time.

Keep trips to his relief area short. Stay no more than five or six minutes and then return to the

KEY TO SUCCESS
Success that comes by luck is usually short-lived. Success that comes by well-thought-out proven methods is often more easily achieved and permanent. This is the

Success Method. It is designed to give you, the puppy owner, a simple yet proven way to help your puppy develop clean living habits and a feeling of security in his new environment.

house. If he goes during that time, praise him lavishly and take him indoors immediately. If he does not, but he has an accident when you go back indoors, pick him up immediately, say 'No! No!' and

HOW MANY TIMES A DAY?

AGE	RELIEF TRIPS
To 14 weeks	10
14–22 weeks	8
22–32 weeks	6
Adulthood	4
(dog stops growing)	

These are estimates, of course, but they are a guide to the MINIMUM opportunities a dog should have each day to relieve itself.

return to his relief area. Wait a few minutes, then return to the house again. Never hit a puppy or rub his face in urine or excrement when he has had an accident!

Once indoors, put the puppy in his crate until you have had time to clean up his accident. Then, release him to the family

THE CLEAN LIFE
By providing sleeping and resting quarters that fit the dog, and offering frequent opportunities to relieve himself outside his quarters, the puppy quickly learns that the outdoors (or the newspaper if you are training him to paper) is the place to go when he needs to urinate or defecate. It also reinforces his innate desire to keep his sleeping quarters clean. This, in turn, helps develop the muscle control that will eventually produce a dog with clean living habits.

area and watch him more closely than before. Chances are, his accident was a result of your not picking up his signal or waiting too long before offering him the opportunity to relieve himself. Never hold a grudge against the puppy for accidents.

Let the puppy learn that going outdoors means it is time to relieve himself, not to play. Once trained, he will be able to play indoors and out and still differentiate between the times for play versus the times for relief.

Help him develop regular hours for naps, being alone, playing by himself and just resting, all in his crate. Encourage him to entertain himself while you are busy with your activities. Let him learn that having you near is comforting, but it is not your main purpose in life to

THE SUCCESS METHOD

6 Steps to Successful Crate Training

1 Tell the puppy 'Crate time!' and place him in the crate with a small treat (a piece of cheese or half of a biscuit). Let him stay in the crate for five minutes while you are in the same room. Then release him and praise lavishly. Never release him when he is fussing. Wait until he is quiet before you let him out.

2 Repeat Step 1 several times a day.

3 The next day, place the puppy in the crate as before. Let him stay there for ten minutes. Do this several times.

4 Continue building time in five-minute increments until the puppy stays in his crate for 30 minutes with you in the room. Always take him to his relief area after prolonged periods in his crate.

5 Now go back to Step 1 and let the puppy stay in his crate for five minutes, this time while you are out of the room.

6 Once again, build crate time in five-minute increments with you out of the room. When the puppy will stay willingly in his crate (he may even fall asleep!) for 30 minutes with you out of the room, he will be ready to stay in it for several hours at a time.

HOUSE-TRAINING TIP
Most of all, be consistent. Always take your dog to the same location, always use the same command and always have the dog on lead when he is in his relief area, unless a fenced-in garden is available.

By following the Success Method, your puppy will be completely house-trained by the time his muscle and brain develop-ment reach maturity. Keep in mind that small breeds usually mature faster than large breeds, but all puppies should be trained by six months of age.

provide him with undivided attention.

Each time you put your puppy in his own area, use the same command, whatever suits best. Soon he will run to his crate or special area when he hears you say those words.

Crate training provides safety for you, the puppy and the home. It also provides the puppy with a feeling of security, and that helps the puppy achieve self-confidence and clean habits. Remember that one of the primary ingredients in house-training your puppy is control. Regardless of your lifestyle, there will always be occasions when you will need to have a place where your dog can stay and be happy and safe. Crate training is the answer for now and in the future.

In conclusion, a few key elements are really all you need for a successful house-training method—consistency, frequency, praise, control and supervision. By following these procedures with a normal, healthy puppy, you and the puppy will soon be past the stage of 'accidents' and ready to move on to a full and rewarding life together.

PLAN TO PLAY
The puppy should also have regular play and exercise sessions when he is with you or a family member. Exercise for a very young puppy can consist of a short walk around the house or garden. Playing can include fetching games with a large ball or a special raggy. (All puppies teethe and need soft things upon which to chew.) Remember to restrict play periods to indoors within his living area (the family room, for example) until he is completely house-trained.

TRAINING RULES

If you want to be successful in training your dog, you have four rules to obey yourself:
1. Develop an understanding of how a dog thinks.
2. Do not blame the dog for lack of communication.
3. Define your dog's personality and act accordingly.
4. Have patience and be consistent.

ROLES OF DISCIPLINE, REWARD AND PUNISHMENT

Discipline, training one to act in accordance with rules, brings order to life. It is as simple as that. Without discipline, particularly in a group society, chaos will reign supreme and the group will eventually perish. Humans and canines are social animals and need some form of discipline in order to function effectively. They must procure food, protect their home base and their young and reproduce to keep their species going. If there were no discipline in the lives of social animals, they would eventually die from starvation and/or predation by other stronger animals.

In the case of domestic canines, discipline in their lives is needed in order for them to understand how their pack (you and other family members) functions and how they must act in order to survive.

A large humane society in a highly populated area recently surveyed dog owners regarding their satisfaction with their relationships with their dogs. People who had trained their dogs were 75% more satisfied with their pets than those who had never trained their dogs.

Dr Edward Thorndike, a psychologist, established *Thorndike's Theory of Learning*, which states that a behaviour that results in a pleasant event tends to be repeated. A behaviour that

Setting limits is a necessary element of training. Gates used as partitions can help to define your dog's designated areas within the home.

results in an unpleasant event tends not to be repeated. It is this theory upon which training methods are based today. For example, if you manipulate a dog to perform a specific behaviour and reward him for doing it, he is likely to do it again because he enjoyed the end result.

Occasionally, punishment, a penalty inflicted for an offence, is necessary. The best type of punishment often comes from an outside source. For example, a child is told not to touch the stove

because he may get burned. He disobeys and touches the stove. In doing so, he receives a burn. From that time on, he respects the heat of the stove and avoids contact with it. Therefore, a behaviour that results in an unpleasant event tends not to be repeated.

A good example of a dog learning the hard way is the dog who chases the house cat. He is told many times to leave the cat alone, yet he persists in teasing the cat. Then, one day, the dog begins chasing the cat but the cat turns and swipes a claw across the

dog's face, leaving the dog with a painful gash on his nose. The final result is that the dog stops chasing the cat. Again, a behaviour that results in an unpleasant event tends not to be repeated.

TRAINING EQUIPMENT

COLLAR AND LEAD
For a Chinese Crested, the collar and lead that you use for training must be one with which you are easily able to work, not too heavy for the dog and perfectly safe.

TREATS
Have a bag of treats on hand; something nutritious and easy to swallow works best. Use a soft treat, a chunk of cheese or a piece of cooked chicken rather than a dry biscuit. By the time the dog has finished chewing a dry treat, he will forget why he is being rewarded in the first place!

Using food rewards will not teach a dog to beg at the table— the only way to teach a dog to beg at the table is to give him food from the table. In training, rewarding the dog with a food treat will help him associate praise and the treats with learning new behaviours that obviously please his owner.

TRAINING BEGINS: ASK THE DOG A QUESTION
In order to teach your dog anything, you must first get his

attention. After all, he cannot learn anything if he is looking away from you with his mind on something else.

To get your dog's attention, ask him 'School?', and immediately walk over to him and give him a treat as you tell him 'Good dog.' Wait a minute or two and repeat the routine, this time with a treat in your hand as you approach within a foot of the dog. Do not go directly to him, but stop about a foot short of him and hold out the treat as you ask 'School?' He will see you approaching with a treat in your hand and most likely begin walking toward you. As you meet, give him the treat and praise again.

The third time, ask the question, have a treat in your hand and walk only a short distance toward the dog so that he must walk almost all the way to you. As he reaches you, give him the treat and praise again.

By this time, the dog will probably be getting the idea that if he pays attention to you, especially when you ask that question, it will pay off in treats and enjoyable activities for him. In other words, he learns that 'school' means doing great things with you that are fun and that result in positive attention for him.

Remember that the dog does not understand your verbal language; he only recognises sounds. Your question translates to a series of sounds for him, and those sounds become the signal to go to you and pay attention. The dog learns that if he does this, he will get to interact with you plus receive treats and praise.

THE BASIC COMMANDS

TEACHING SIT

Now that you have the dog's attention, attach his lead and hold it in your left hand, and hold a

OPEN MINDS
Dogs are as different from each other as people are. What works for one dog may not work for another. Have an open mind. If one method of training is unsuccessful, try another.

food treat in your right hand. Place your food hand at the dog's nose and let him lick the treat but not take it from you. Say 'Sit' and slowly raise your food hand from in front of the dog's nose up over his head so that he is looking at the ceiling. As he bends his head upward, he will have to bend his knees to maintain his balance. As he bends his knees, he will assume a sit position. At that point, release the food treat and praise lavishly with comments such as 'Good dog! Good sit!,' etc. Remember to always praise enthusiastically, because dogs relish verbal praise from their owners and feel so proud of

themselves whenever they accomplish a behaviour.

You will not use food forever in getting the dog to obey your commands. Food is only used to teach new behaviours and, once the dog knows what you want when you give a specific command, you will wean him off the food treats but still maintain the verbal praise. After all, you will always have your voice with you, and there will be many times when you have no food rewards but expect the dog to obey.

TEACHING DOWN

Teaching the down exercise is easy when you understand how

You may have to gently coax your Crested into the sit position the first few times, but he should catch on in no time.

the dog perceives the down position, and it is very difficult when you do not. Dogs perceive the down position as a submissive one; therefore, teaching the down exercise by using a forceful method can sometimes make the dog develop such a fear of the down that he either runs away when you say 'Down' or he attempts to snap at the person who tries to force him down.

Have the dog sit close alongside your left leg, facing in the same direction as you are. Hold the lead in your left hand and a food treat in your right. Now place your left hand lightly on the top of the dog's shoulders where they meet above the spinal cord. Do not push down on the dog's shoulders; simply rest your left hand there so you can guide the dog to lie down close to your left leg rather than to swing away from your side when he drops.

Now place the food hand at the dog's nose, say 'Down' very softly (almost a whisper), and slowly lower the food hand to the dog's front feet. When the food hand reaches the floor, begin moving it forward along the floor in front of the dog. Keep talking softly to the dog, saying things like, 'Do you want this treat? You can do this, good dog.' Your reassuring tone of voice will help calm the dog as he tries to follow the food hand in order to get the treat.

DOUBLE JEOPARDY
A dog in jeopardy never lies down. He stays alert on his feet because instinct tells him that he may have to run away or fight for his survival. Therefore, if a dog feels threatened or anxious, he will not lie down. Consequently, it is important to have the dog calm and relaxed as he learns the down exercise.

When the dog's elbows touch the floor, release the food and praise softly. Try to get the dog to maintain that down position for several seconds before you let him sit up again. The goal here is to get the dog to settle down and not feel threatened in the down position.

CONSISTENCY PAYS OFF

Dogs need consistency in their feeding schedule, exercise and toilet breaks, and in the verbal commands you use. If you use 'Stay' on Monday and 'Stay here, please' on Tuesday, you will confuse your dog. Don't demand perfect behaviour during training classes and then let him have the run of the house the rest of the day. Above all, lavish praise on your pet consistently every time he does something right. The more he feels he is pleasing you, the more willing he will be to learn.

TEACHING STAY

It is easy to teach the dog to stay in either a sit or a down position. Again, we use food and praise during the teaching process as we help the dog to understand exactly what it is that we are expecting him to do.

To teach the sit/stay, start with the dog sitting on your left side as before and hold the lead in your left hand. Have a food treat in your right hand and place your food hand at the dog's nose. Say 'Stay' and step out on your right foot to stand directly in front of the dog, toe to toe, as he licks and nibbles the treat. Be sure to keep his head facing upward to maintain the sit position. Count to five and then swing around to stand next to the dog again with him on your left. As soon as you get back to the original position, release the food and praise lavishly.

To teach the down/stay, do the down as previously described. As soon as the dog lies down, say 'Stay' and step out on your right foot just as you did in the sit/stay. Count to five and then return to stand beside the dog with him on your left side. Release the treat and praise as always.

Within a week or ten days, you can begin to add a bit of distance between you and your dog when you leave him. When you do, use your left hand open with the palm facing the dog as a

FEAR AGGRESSION

Pups who are subjected to physical abuse during training commonly end up with behavioural problems as adults. One common result of abuse is fear aggression, in which a dog will lash out, bare his teeth, snarl and finally bite someone by whom he feels threatened. For example, your daughter may be playing with the dog one afternoon. As they play hide-and-seek, she backs the dog into a corner and, as she attempts to tease him playfully, he bites her hand. Examine the cause of this behaviour. Did your daughter ever hit the dog? Did someone who resembles your daughter hit or scream at the dog?

Fortunately, fear aggression is relatively easy to correct. Have your daughter engage in only positive activities with the dog, such as feeding, petting and walking. She should not give any corrections or negative feedback. If the dog still growls or cowers away from her, allow someone else to accompany them. After approximately one week, the dog should feel that he can rely on her for many positive things, and he will also be prevented from reacting fearfully towards anyone who might resemble her.

stay signal, much the same as the hand signal a constable uses to stop traffic at an intersection. Hold the food treat in your right hand as before, but this time the food will not be touching the dog's nose. He will watch the food hand and quickly learn that he is going to get that treat as soon as you return to his side.

When you can stand 1 metre away from your dog for 30 seconds, you can then begin building time and distance in both stays. Eventually, the dog can be expected to remain in the stay position for prolonged periods of time until you return to him or call him to you. Always praise lavishly when he stays.

TEACHING COME

If you make teaching 'come' an exciting experience, you should never have a 'student' that does not love the game or that fails to come when called. The secret, it seems, is never to teach the word 'come.'

At times when an owner most wants his dog to come when called, the owner is likely to be upset or anxious and he allows these feelings to come through in the tone of his voice when he calls his dog. Hearing that desperation in his owner's voice, the dog fears the results of going to him and therefore either disobeys outright or runs in the opposite direction. The secret, therefore, is to teach the dog a game and, when you want him to come to you, simply play the game. It is practically a no-fail solution!

To begin, have several members of your family take a few food treats and each go into a different room in the house. Everyone takes turns calling the dog, and each person should celebrate the dog's finding him with a treat and lots of happy praise. When a person calls the dog, he is actually inviting the dog to find him and to get a treat as a reward for 'winning.'

A few turns of the 'Where are you?' game and the dog will understand that everyone is playing the game and that each person has a big celebration awaiting the dog's success at

'WHERE ARE YOU?'
When calling the dog, do not say 'Come.' Say things like, 'Rover, where are you? See if you can find me! I have a biscuit for you!' Keep up a constant line of chatter with coaxing sounds and frequent questions such as, 'Where are you?' The dog will learn to follow the sound of your voice to locate you and receive his reward.

'COME'. . . BACK
Never call your dog to come to you for a correction or scold him when he reaches you. That is the quickest way to turn a 'Come' command into 'Go away fast!' Dogs think only in the present tense, and your dog will connect the scolding with coming to you, not with the misbehaviour of a few moments earlier.

locating him or her. Once the dog learns to love the game, simply calling out 'Where are you?' will bring him running from wherever he is when he hears that all-important question.

The come command is recognised as one of the most important things to teach a dog, but there are trainers who work with thousands of dogs and never teach the actual word 'Come.' Yet these dogs will race to respond to a person who uses the dog's name followed by 'Where are you?' For example, a woman has a 12-year-old companion dog who went blind, but who never fails to locate her owner when asked, 'Where are you?'

Children, in particular, love to play this game with their dogs. Children can hide in smaller places like a shower or bath, behind a bed or under a table. The dog needs to work a little bit harder to find these hiding places, but, when he does, he loves to celebrate with a treat and a tussle with a favourite youngster.

TEACHING HEEL

Heeling means that the dog walks beside the owner without pulling. It takes time and patience on the owner's part to succeed at teaching the dog that he (the owner) will not proceed unless the dog is walking calmly beside him. Neither pulling out ahead on the lead nor lagging behind is acceptable.

Begin by holding the lead in your left hand as the dog sits beside your left leg. Move the

loop end of the lead to your right hand, but keep your left hand short on the lead so that it keeps the dog in close next to you.

Say 'Heel' and step forward

To teach any command, you must have your dog's complete attention. Do not attempt to train your dog in areas that hold many distractions.

SAFETY FIRST

While it may seem that the most important things to your dog are eating, sleeping and chewing the upholstery on your furniture, his first concern is actually safety. The domesticated dogs we keep as companions have the same pack instinct as their ancestors who ran free thousands of years ago. Because of this pack instinct, your dog wants to know that he and his pack are not in danger of being harmed, and that his pack has a strong, capable leader. You must establish yourself as the leader early on in your relationship. That way your dog will trust that you will take care of him and the pack, and he will accept your commands without question.

TUG OF WALK?

If you begin teaching the heel by taking long walks and letting the dog pull you along, he misinterprets this action as an acceptable form of taking a walk. When you pull back on the lead to counteract his pulling, he reads that tug as a signal to pull even harder!

on your left foot. Keep the dog close to you and take three steps. Stop and have the dog sit next to you in what we now call the 'heel position.' Praise verbally, but do not touch the dog. Hesitate a moment and begin again with 'Heel,' taking three steps and stopping, at which point the dog is told to sit again.

Your goal here is to have the dog walk those three steps without pulling on the lead. Once he will walk calmly beside you for three steps without pulling, increase the number of steps you take to five. When he will walk politely beside you while you take five steps, you can increase the length of your walk to ten steps. Keep increasing the length of your

stroll until the dog will walk quietly beside you without pulling as long as you want him to heel. When you stop heeling, indicate to the dog that the exercise is over by verbally praising as you pet him and say 'OK, good dog.' The 'OK' is used as a release word, meaning that the exercise is finished and the dog is free to relax.

If you are dealing with a dog who insists on pulling you around, simply 'put on your brakes' and stand your ground until the dog realises that the two of you are not going anywhere until he is beside you and moving

The great outdoors may present too many enticing smells, sounds and other sensations to be a viable place to practise heel training with your Crested.

TRAINING TIP
If you are walking your dog and he suddenly stops and looks straight into your eyes, ignore him. Pull the leash and lead him into the direction you want to walk.

HEELING WELL

Teach your dog to heel in an enclosed area. Once you think the dog will obey reliably and you want to attempt advanced obedience exercises such as off-lead heeling, test him in a fenced-in area so he cannot run away.

A well-'heeled' Crested struts his stuff on the end of the lead in the show ring.

at your pace, not his. It may take some time just standing there to convince the dog that you are the leader and that you will be the one to decide on the direction and

KEEP SMILING

Never train your dog, puppy or adult, when you are angry or in a sour mood. Dogs are very sensitive to human feelings, especially anger, and if your dog senses that you are angry or upset, he will connect your anger with his training and learn to resent or fear his training sessions.

speed of your travel.

Each time the dog looks up at you or slows down to give a slack lead between the two of you, quietly praise him and say, 'Good heel. Good dog.' Eventually, the dog will begin to respond and within a few days he will be walking politely beside you without pulling on the lead. At first, the training sessions should be kept short and very positive; soon the dog will be able to walk nicely with you for increasingly longer distances. Remember also to give the dog free time and the opportunity to run and play when you have finished heel practice.

OBEDIENCE CLASSES

A basic obedience beginner's class usually lasts for six to eight weeks. Dog and owner attend an hour-long lesson once a week and practise for a few minutes, several times a day, each day at home. If done properly, the whole procedure will result in a well-mannered dog and an owner who delights in living with a pet that is eager to please and enjoys doing things with his owner.

WEANING OFF FOOD IN TRAINING

Food is used in training new behaviours. Once the dog understands what behaviour goes with a specific command, it is time to start weaning him off the food treats. At first, give a treat after each exercise. Then, start to give a treat only after every other exercise. Mix up the times when you offer a food reward and the times when you only offer praise so that the dog will never know when he is going to receive both food and praise and when he is going to receive only praise. This is called a variable ratio reward system. It proves successful because there is always the chance that the owner will produce a treat, so the dog never stops trying for that reward. ALWAYS give verbal praise.

OBEDIENCE CLASSES

It is a good idea to enrol in an obedience class if one is available in your area. If yours is a show dog, ringcraft classes would be more appropriate. Many areas have dog clubs that offer basic obedience training as well as preparatory classes for obedience competition. There are also local dog trainers who offer similar classes. Some Chinese Cresteds do participate in basic obedience competition.

At obedience shows, dogs can earn titles at various levels of competition. The beginning levels of obedience competition include basic behaviours such as sit, down, heel, etc. The more advanced levels of competition include jumping, retrieving, scent discrimination and signal work.

DID YOU KNOW?

Occasionally, a dog and owner who have not attended formal classes have been able to earn entry-level titles by obtaining competition rules and regulations from a local kennel club and practising on their own to a degree of perfection. Obtaining the higher level titles, however, almost always requires extensive training under the tutelage of experienced instructors. In addition, the more difficult levels require more specialised equipment whereas the lower levels do not.

OBEDIENCE SCHOOL

Taking your dog to an obedience school may be the best investment in time and money you can ever make. You will enjoy the benefits for the lifetime of your dog and you will have the opportunity to meet people who have similar expectations for their companion dogs.

The advanced levels require a dog and owner to put a lot of time and effort into their training. The titles that can be earned at these levels of competition are very prestigious.

OTHER ACTIVITIES FOR LIFE

Whether a dog is trained in the structured environment of a class or alone with his owner at home, there are many activities that can bring fun and rewards to both owner and dog once they have mastered basic control.

Teaching the dog to help out around the home, in the garden or on the farm provides great satisfaction to both dog and owner. In addition, the dog's help makes life a little easier for his owner and raises his stature as a valued companion to his family. It helps give the dog a purpose by occupying his mind and providing an outlet for his energy.

If you are interested in participating in organised competition with your Chinese Crested, there are activities other than obedience in which you and your dog can become involved. Agility is a popular sport in which dogs run through an obstacle course that includes various jumps, tunnels and other exercises to test the dog's speed and coordination. Mini-agility has been devised by The Kennel Club for small breeds. The events are essentially the same, except all obstacles have been reduced in size so that small dogs can participate. The owners run beside their dogs to give commands and to guide them through the course. Although competitive, the focus is on fun—it's fun to do, fun to watch and great exercise.

A successful day in the ring for both dog and owner.

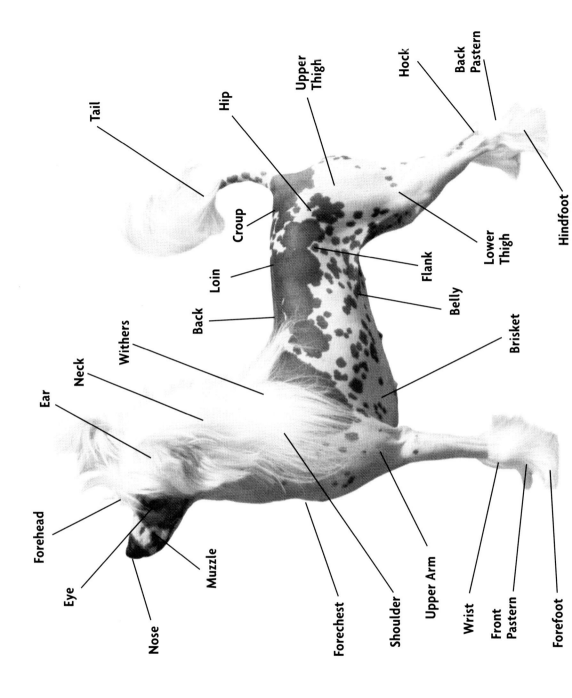

Tail

Hip

Upper Thigh

Hock

Back Pastern

Croup

Loin

Back

Withers

Neck

Ear

Forehead

Eye

Nose

Muzzle

Forechest

Shoulder

Upper Arm

Flank

Lower Thigh

Belly

Brisket

Hindfoot

Wrist

Front Pastern

Forefoot

PHYSICAL STRUCTURE OF THE CHINESE CRESTED

Dogs suffer from many of the same physical illnesses as people. They might even share many of the same psychological problems. Since people usually know more about human diseases than canine maladies, many of the terms used in this chapter will be familiar but not necessarily those used by veterinary surgeons. We will use the term *x-ray*, instead of the more acceptable term *radiograph*. We will also use the familiar term *symptoms* even though dogs don't have symptoms, which are verbal descriptions of the patient's feelings; dogs have *clinical signs*. Since dogs can't speak, we have to look for clinical signs...but we still use the term *symptoms* in this book.

As a general rule, medicine is *practised*. That term is not arbitrary. Medicine is a constantly changing art as we learn more and more about genetics, electronic aids (like CAT scans) and daily laboratory advances. There are many dog maladies, like canine hip dysplasia, which are not universally treated in the same manner. Some veterinary surgeons opt for surgery more often than others do.

SELECTING A VETERINARY SURGEON

Your selection of a veterinary surgeon should not be based upon personality (as most are) but upon their convenience to your home. You want a vet who is close because you might have emergencies or need to make multiple visits for treatments. You want a vet who has services that you might require such as tattooing and grooming, as well as sophisticated pet supplies and a good reputation for ability and responsiveness. There is nothing more frustrating than having to wait a day or more to get a response from your veterinary surgeon.

All veterinary surgeons are licensed and their diplomas and/or certificates should be displayed in their waiting rooms. There are, however, many veterinary specialities that usually require further studies and internships. There are specialists in heart problems (veterinary cardiologists), skin problems (veterinary dermatologists), teeth and gum problems (veterinary dentists), eye problems (veterinary ophthalmologists) and x-rays (veterinary radiologists), as well

1. Oesophagus
2. Lungs
3. Gall Bladder
4. Liver
5. Kidney
6. Stomach
7. Intestines
8. Urinary Bladder

INTERNAL ORGANS OF THE CHINESE CRESTED

as vets who have specialities in bones, muscles or other organs. Most veterinary surgeons do routine surgery such as neutering, stitching up wounds and docking tails for those breeds in which such is required for show purposes. When the problem affecting your dog is serious, it is not unusual or impudent to get another medical opinion, although in Britain you are obliged to advise the vets concerned about this. You might also want to compare costs among several veterinary surgeons. Sophisticated health care and

Breakdown of Veterinary Income by Category

%	Category
2%	Dentistry
4%	Radiology
12%	Surgery
15%	Vaccinations
19%	Laboratory
23%	Examinations
25%	Medicines

A typical American vet's income, categorised according to services performed. This survey dealt with small-animal (pets) practices.

Vitamins Recommended for Dogs

Some breeders and vets recommend the supplementation of vitamins to a dog's diet—others do not. Before embarking on a vitamin programme, consult your vet.

Vitamin / Dosage	Food source	Benefits
A / 10,000 IU/week	Eggs, butter, yoghurt, meat	Skin, eyes, hind legs, haircoat
B / Varies	Organs, cottage cheese, sardines	Appetite, fleas, heart, skin and coat
C / 2000 mg+	Fruit, legumes, leafy green vegetables	Healing, arthritis, kidneys
D / Varies	Cod liver, cheese, organs, eggs	Bones, teeth, endocrine system
E / 250 IU daily	Leafy green vegetables, meat, wheat germ oil	Skin, muscles, nerves, healing, digestion
F / Varies	Fish oils, raw meat	Heart, skin, coat, fleas
K / Varies	Naturally in body, not through food	Blood clotting

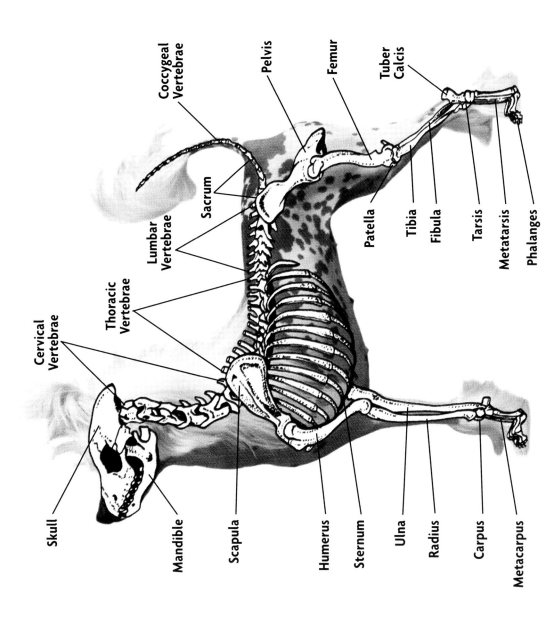

Coccygeal Vertebrae
Pelvis
Femur
Tuber Calcis
Sacrum
Lumbar Vertebrae
Patella
Tibia
Fibula
Tarsis
Metatarsis
Phalanges
Thoracic Vertebrae
Cervical Vertebrae
Skull
Mandible
Scapula
Humerus
Sternum
Ulna
Radius
Carpus
Metacarpus

SKELETAL STRUCTURE OF THE CHINESE CRESTED

veterinary services can be very costly. It is not infrequent that important decisions are based upon financial considerations.

PREVENTATIVE MEDICINE

It is much easier, less costly and more effective to practise preventative medicine than to fight bouts of illness and disease. Properly bred puppies come from parents who were selected based upon their genetic disease profile. Their mothers should have been vaccinated, free of all internal and external parasites and properly nourished. For these reasons, a

visit to the veterinary surgeon who cared for the dam is recommended. The dam can pass on disease resistance to her puppies, which can last for eight to ten weeks. She can also pass on parasites and many infections. That's why you should visit the veterinary surgeon who cared for the dam.

VACCINATION SCHEDULING

Most vaccinations are given by injection and should only be done by a veterinary surgeon. Both he and you should keep a record of the date of the injection, the

DISEASE REFERENCE CHART

	What is it?	What causes it?	Symptoms
Leptospirosis	Severe disease that affects the internal organs; can be spread to people.	A bacterium, which is often carried by rodents, that enters through mucous membranes and spreads quickly throughout the body.	Range from fever, vomiting and loss of appetite in less severe cases to shock, irreversible kidney damage and possibly death in most severe cases.
Rabies	Potentially deadly virus that infects warm-blooded mammals. Not seen in United Kingdom.	Bite from a carrier of the virus, mainly wild animals.	1st stage: dog exhibits change in behaviour, fear. 2nd stage: dog's behaviour becomes more aggressive. 3rd stage: loss of coordination, trouble with bodily functions.
Parvovirus	Highly contagious virus, potentially deadly.	Ingestion of the virus, which is usually spread through the faeces of infected dogs.	Most common: severe diarrhoea. Also vomiting, fatigue, lack of appetite.
Kennel cough	Contagious respiratory infection.	Combination of types of bacteria and virus. Most common: *Bordetella bronchiseptica* bacteria and parainfluenza virus.	Chronic cough.
Distemper	Disease primarily affecting respiratory and nervous system.	Virus that is related to the human measles virus.	Mild symptoms such as fever, lack of appetite and mucous secretion progress to evidence of brain damage, 'hard pad.'
Hepatitis	Virus primarily affecting the liver.	Canine adenovirus type I (CAV-1). Enters system when dog breathes in particles.	Lesser symptoms include listlessness, diarrhoea, vomiting. More severe symptoms include 'blue-eye' (clumps of virus in eye).
Coronavirus	Virus resulting in digestive problems.	Virus is spread through infected dog's faeces.	Stomach upset evidenced by lack of appetite, vomiting, diarrhoea.

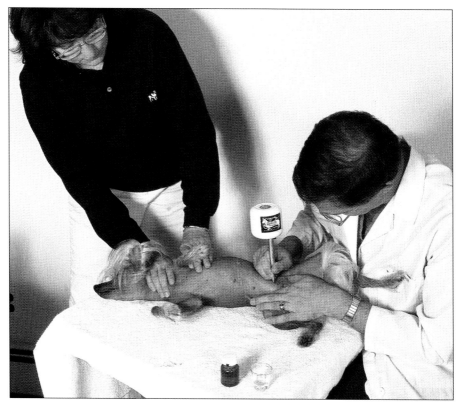

(Above) It is helpful if your vet can perform additional services such as tattooing. (Below) The vet is not just your dog's doctor, but his dentist as well. Your dog should have routine dental exams just as you do.

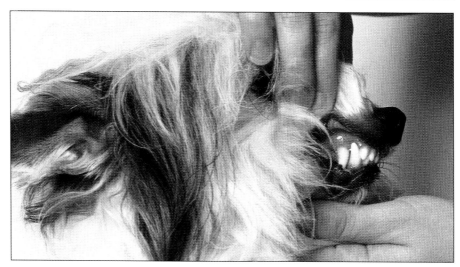

VACCINE ALLERGIES
Vaccines do not work all the time. Sometimes dogs are allergic to them and many times the antibodies, which are supposed to be stimulated by the vaccine, just are not produced. You should keep your dog in the veterinary clinic for an hour after it is vaccinated to be sure there are no allergic reactions.

identification of the vaccine and the amount given. Some vets give a first vaccination at eight weeks, but most dog breeders prefer the course not to commence until about ten weeks because of negating any antibodies passed on by the dam. The vaccination scheduling is usually based on a 15-day cycle. You must take your vet's advice regarding when to vaccinate as this may differ according to the vaccine used. Most vaccinations immunize your puppy against viruses.

The usual vaccines contain immunizing doses of several different viruses such as distemper, parvovirus, parainfluenza and hepatitis, although some veterinary surgeons recommend separate vaccines for each disease. There are other vaccines available when the puppy is at risk. You should rely upon professional advice. This is especially true for the booster-shot programme. Most vaccination

programmes require a booster when the puppy is a year old and once a year thereafter. In some cases, circumstances may require more or less frequent immunizations. Kennel cough, more formally known as tracheobronchitis, is treated with a vaccine that is sprayed into the dog's nostrils. Kennel cough is usually included in routine vaccination, but this is often not so effective as for other major diseases.

WEANING TO FIVE MONTHS OLD
Puppies should be weaned by the time they are about two months old. A puppy that remains for at least eight weeks with its mother and littermates usually adapts better to other dogs and people later in its life.

Some new owners have their puppy examined by a veterinary surgeon immediately, which is a good idea. Vaccination programmes usually begin when the puppy is very young.

MORE THAN VACCINES
Vaccinations help prevent your new puppy from contracting diseases, but they do not cure them. Proper nutrition as well as parasite control keep your dog healthy and less susceptible to many dangerous diseases. Remember that your dog depends on you to ensure his well-being.

The puppy will have its teeth examined and have its skeletal conformation and general health checked prior to certification by the veterinary surgeon. Puppies in certain breeds have problems with their kneecaps, cataracts and other eye problems, heart murmurs and undescended testicles. They may also have personality problems and your veterinary surgeon might have training in temperament evaluation.

FIVE TO TWELVE MONTHS OF AGE
Unless you intend to breed or show your dog, neutering the puppy at six months of age is recommended. Discuss this with your veterinary surgeon. Neutering has proven to be extremely beneficial to both male and female puppies. Besides eliminating the possibility of pregnancy, it inhibits (but does not prevent) breast cancer in bitches and prostate cancer in male dogs. Under no circumstances should a bitch be spayed prior to her first season.

Your veterinary surgeon should provide your puppy with a thorough dental evaluation at six months of age, ascertaining whether all the permanent teeth have erupted properly. A home

HEALTH AND VACCINATION SCHEDULE

AGE IN WEEKS:	6TH	8TH	10TH	12TH	14TH	16TH	20-24TH	1 YR
Worm Control	✔	✔	✔	✔	✔	✔	✔	
Neutering								✔
Heartworm		✔		✔		✔	✔	
Parvovirus	✔		✔		✔		✔	✔
Distemper		✔		✔		✔		✔
Hepatitis		✔		✔		✔		✔
Leptospirosis								✔
Parainfluenza	✔		✔		✔			✔
Dental Examination		✔					✔	✔
Complete Physical		✔					✔	✔
Coronavirus				✔			✔	✔
Kennel Cough	✔							
Hip Dysplasia								✔
Rabies							✔	

Vaccinations are not instantly effective. It takes about two weeks for the dog's immune system to develop antibodies. Most vaccinations require annual booster shots. Your veterinary surgeon should guide you in this regard.

DON'T EAT THE DAISIES!

Many plants and flowers are beautiful to look at, but can be highly toxic if ingested by your dog. Reactions range from abdominal pain and vomiting to convulsions and death. If the following plants are in your home, remove them. If they are outside your house or in your garden, avoid accidents by making sure your dog is never left unsupervised in those locations.

Azalea	Dumb cane	Mescal bean
Belladonna	Dutchman's breeches	Mushrooms
Bird of Paradise	Elephant's ear	Nightshade
Bulbs	Hydrangea	Philodendron
Calla lily	Jack-in-the-pulpit	Poinsettia
Cardinal flower	Jasmine	*Prunus* species
Castor bean	Jimsonweed	Tobacco
Chinaberry tree	Larkspur	Yellow jasmine
Daphne	Laurel	Yews, *Taxus* species
	Lily of the valley	

dental care regimen should be initiated at six months, including brushing weekly and providing good dental devices (such as nylon bones). Regular dental care promotes healthy teeth, fresh breath and a longer life.

ONE TO SEVEN YEARS
Once a year, your grown dog should visit the vet for an examination and vaccination boosters, if needed. Some vets recommend blood tests, thyroid level check and dental evaluation to accompany these annual visits. A thorough clinical evaluation by the vet can provide critical background information for your dog. Blood tests are often performed at one year of age, and dental examinations around the third or fourth birthday. In the long run, quality preventative care for your pet can save money, teeth and lives.

SKIN PROBLEMS IN CHINESE CRESTEDS
Veterinary surgeons are consulted by dog owners for skin problems more than any other group of diseases or maladies. Dogs' skin is almost as sensitive as human skin and both suffer almost the same ailments. Chinese Cresteds are even known to suffer from acne. For this reason, veterinary

dermatology has developed into a speciality practised by many veterinary surgeons.

Since many skin problems have visual symptoms that are almost identical, it requires the skill of an experienced veterinary dermatologist to identify and cure many of the more severe skin disorders. Pet shops sell many treatments for skin problems but most of the treatments are directed at symptoms and not the underlying problem(s). If your dog is suffering from a skin disorder, you should seek professional assistance as quickly as possible. As with all diseases, the earlier a problem is identified and treated, the more successful is the cure.

PARASITE BITES

Many of us are allergic to insect bites. The bites itch, erupt and may even become infected. Dogs have the same reaction to fleas, ticks and/or mites. When an insect lands on you, you have the chance to whisk it away with your hand. Unfortunately, when your dog is bitten by a flea, tick or mite, it can only scratch it away or bite it. By the time the dog has been bitten, the parasite has done some of its damage. It may also have laid eggs to cause further problems in the near future. The itching from parasite bites is probably due to the saliva injected into the site when the parasite sucks the dog's blood.

AUTO-IMMUNE SKIN CONDITIONS

Auto-immune skin conditions are commonly referred to as being allergic to yourself, while allergies are usually inflammatory reactions to an outside stimulus. Auto-immune diseases cause serious damage to the tissues that are involved.

The best known auto-immune disease is lupus, which affects people as well as dogs. The symptoms are variable and may affect the kidneys, bones, blood chemistry and skin. It can be fatal to both dogs and humans, though it is not thought to be transmissible. It is usually successfully treated with cortisone, prednisone or a similar corticosteroid, but extensive use of these drugs can have harmful side effects.

AIRBORNE ALLERGIES

An interesting allergy is pollen allergy. Humans have hay fever, rose fever and other fevers with which they suffer during the pollinating season. Many dogs suffer the same allergies. When the pollen count is high, your dog might suffer but don't expect him to sneeze and have a runny nose like humans. Dogs react to pollen allergies the same way they react to fleas—they scratch and bite themselves.

Dogs, like humans, can be tested for allergens. Discuss the testing with your veterinary dermatologist.

FOOD PROBLEMS

FOOD ALLERGIES

Dogs are allergic to many foods that are best-sellers and highly recommended by breeders and veterinary surgeons. Changing the brand of food that you buy may not eliminate the problem if the element to which the dog is allergic is contained in the new brand.

Recognising a food allergy is difficult. Humans vomit or have rashes when they eat a food to which they are allergic. Dogs neither vomit nor (usually) develop a rash. They react in the same manner as they do to an airborne or flea allergy; they itch, scratch and bite, thus making the diagnosis extremely difficult. While pollen allergies and parasite bites are usually seasonal, food allergies are year-round problems.

FOOD INTOLERANCE

Food intolerance is the inability of the dog to completely digest certain foods. Puppies that may have done very well on their mother's milk may not do well on cow's milk. The result of this food intolerance may be loose bowels, passing gas and stomach pains. These are the only obvious symptoms of food intolerance and that makes diagnosis difficult.

TREATING FOOD PROBLEMS

It is possible to handle food allergies and food intolerance yourself. Put your dog on a diet that it has never had. Obviously, if it has never eaten this new food, it can't have been allergic or intolerant of it. Start with a single ingredient that is not in the dog's diet at the present time. Ingredients like chopped beef or fish are common in dogs' diets, so try something more exotic like rabbit, pheasant or even just vegetables. Keep the dog on this diet (with no additives) for a month. If the symptoms of food allergy or intolerance disappear, chances are your dog has a food allergy.

Don't think that the single ingredient cured the problem. You still must find a suitable diet and ascertain which ingredient in the old diet was objectionable. This is most easily done by adding ingredients to the new diet one at a time. Let the dog stay on the modified diet for a month before you add another ingredient. Eventually, you will determine the ingredient that caused the adverse reaction.

An alternative method is to carefully study the ingredients in the diet to which your dog is allergic or intolerant. Identify the main ingredient in this diet and eliminate the main ingredient by buying a different food that does not have that ingredient. Keep experimenting until the symptoms disappear after one month on the new diet.

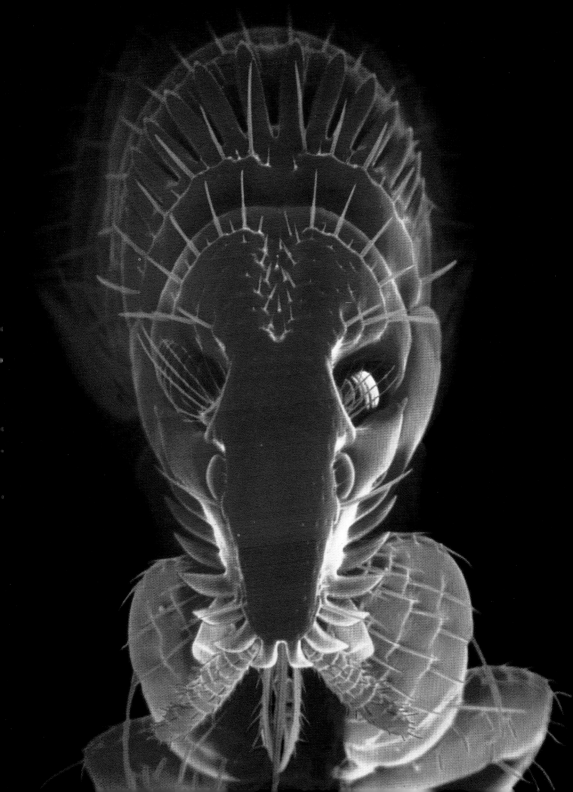

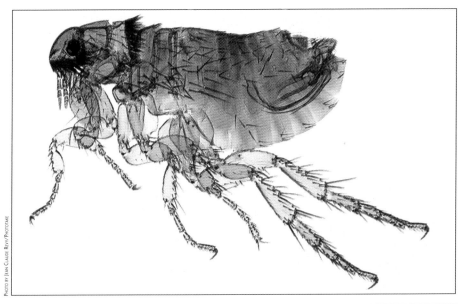

PHOTO BY JEAN CLAUDE REVY/PHOTOTAKE

A male dog flea, *Ctenocephalides canis.*

EXTERNAL PARASITES

FLEAS
Of all the problems to which dogs are prone, none is more well known and frustrating than fleas, especially for Powder Puffs. Flea infestation is relatively simple to cure but difficult to prevent. Parasites that are harboured inside the body are a bit more difficult to eradicate but they are easier to control.

To control flea infestation, you have to understand the flea's life cycle. Fleas are often thought of as a summertime problem, but centrally heated homes have changed the patterns and fleas can be found at any time of the year. The most effective method of flea control is a two-stage approach:

S.E.M. BY DR DENNIS KUNKEL, UNIVERSITY OF HAWAII

Magnified head of a dog flea, *Ctenocephalides canis.*

one stage to kill the adult fleas, and the other to control the development of pre-adult fleas. Unfortunately, no single active ingredient is effective against all stages of the life cycle.

LIFE CYCLE STAGES
During its life, a flea will pass through four life stages: egg, larva, pupa and adult. The adult stage is the most visible and irritating stage

Opposite page: A scanning electron micrograph of a dog or cat flea, *Ctenocephalides,* magnified more than 100x. This image has been colorized for effect.

The Life Cycle of the Flea

Eggs

Larvae

Pupa

Adult

Photos courtesy of Fleabusters®, Rx for Fleas.

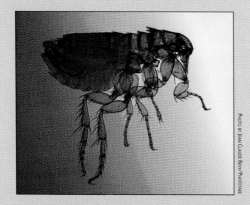

Photo by Jean Claude Revy/Phototake

A LOOK AT FLEAS

Fleas have been around for millions of years and have adapted to changing host animals. They are able to go through a complete life cycle in less than one month or they can extend their lives to almost two years by remaining as pupae or cocoons. They do not need blood or any other food for up to 20 months.

They have been measured as being able to jump 300,000 times and can jump 150 times their length in any direction, including straight up. Those are just a few of the reasons why they are so successful in infesting a dog!

of the flea life cycle, and this is why the majority of flea-control products concentrate on this stage. The fact is that adult fleas account for only 1% of the total flea population, and the other 99% exist in pre-adult stages, i.e. eggs, larvae and pupae. The pre-adult stages are barely visible to the naked eye.

THE LIFE CYCLE OF THE FLEA

Eggs are laid on the dog, usually in quantities of about 20 or 30, several times a day. The female adult flea must have a blood meal before each egg-laying session. When first laid, the eggs will cling to the dog's hair, as the eggs are still moist. However, they will quickly dry out and fall from the dog, especially if the dog moves around or scratches. Many eggs will fall off in the dog's favourite area or an area in which he spends a lot of time, such as his bed.

Once the eggs fall from the dog onto the carpet or furniture, they will hatch into larvae. This takes from one to ten days. Larvae are not particularly mobile and will usually travel only a few inches from where they hatch. However, they do have a tendency to move away from light and heavy traffic—under furniture and behind doors are common places to find high quantities of flea larvae.

The flea larvae feed on dead organic matter, including adult flea faeces, until they are ready to change into adult fleas. Fleas will usually remain as larvae for around seven days. After this period, the larvae will pupate into protective pupae. While inside the pupae, the larvae will undergo metamorphosis and change into adult fleas. This can take as little time as a few days, but the adult fleas can remain inside the pupae waiting to hatch for up to two years. The pupae are signalled to hatch by certain stimuli, such as physical pressure—the pupae's being stepped on, heat from an animal lying on the pupae or increased carbon dioxide levels and vibrations—indicating that a suitable host is available.

FLEA KILLERS

Flea-killers are poisonous. You should not spray these toxic chemicals on areas of a dog's body that he licks, on his genitals or on his face. Flea killers taken internally are a better answer, but check with your vet in case internal therapy is not advised for your dog.

INSECT GROWTH REGULATOR (IGR)

Two types of products should be used when treating fleas—a product to treat the pet and a product to treat the home. Adult fleas represent less than 1% of the flea population. The pre-adult fleas (eggs, larvae and pupae) represent more than 99% of the flea population and are found in the environment; it is in the case of pre-adult fleas that products containing an Insect Growth Regulator (IGR) should be used in the home.

IGRs are a new class of compounds used to prevent the development of insects. They do not kill the insect outright, but instead use the insect's biology against it to stop it from completing its growth. Products that contain methoprene are the world's first and leading IGRs. Used to control fleas and other insects, this type of IGR will stop flea larvae from developing and protect the house for up to seven months.

Once hatched, the adult flea must feed within a few days. Once the adult flea finds a host, it will not leave voluntarily. It only becomes dislodged by grooming or the host animal's scratching. The adult flea will remain on the host for the duration of its life unless forcibly removed.

A scanning electron micrograph (S. E. M.) of a dog flea, *Ctenocephalides canis*.

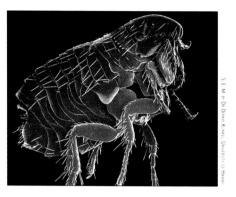

TREATING THE ENVIRONMENT AND THE DOG

Treating fleas should be a two-pronged attack. First, the environment needs to be treated; this includes carpets and furniture, especially the dog's bedding and areas underneath furniture. The environment should be treated with a household spray containing an Insect Growth Regulator (IGR) and an insecticide to kill the adult fleas. Most IGRs are effective against eggs and larvae; they

Dwight R Kuhn's magnificent action photo, showing a flea jumping from a dog's back.

actually mimic the fleas' own hormones and stop the eggs and larvae from developing into adult fleas. There are currently no treatments available to attack the pupa stage of the life cycle, so the adult insecticide is used to kill the newly hatched adult fleas before they find a host. Most IGRs are active for many months, while adult insecticides are only active for a few days.

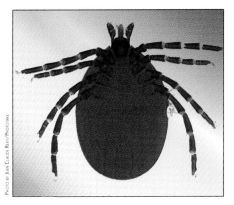

An uncommon dog tick of the genus *Ixode*. Magnified 10x.

PHOTO BY JEAN CLAUDE REVY/PHOTOTAKE

When treating with a household spray, it is a good idea to vacuum before applying the product. This stimulates as many pupae as possible to hatch into adult fleas. The vacuum cleaner should also be treated with an

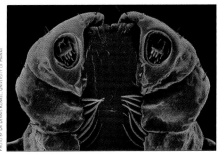

PHOTO BY DR DENNIS KUNKEL, UNIVERSITY OF HAWAII

insecticide to prevent the eggs and larvae that have been hoovered into the vacuum bag from hatching.

The second stage of treatment is to apply an adult insecticide to the dog. Traditionally, this would be in the form of a collar or a spray, but more recent innovations include digestible insecticides that poison the fleas when they ingest the dog's blood. Alternatively, there are drops that, when placed on the back of the animal's neck, spread throughout the fur and skin to kill adult fleas.

TICKS AND MITES

Though not as common as fleas, ticks and mites are found all over the tropical and temperate world. They don't bite, like fleas; they harpoon. They dig their sharp proboscis (nose) into the dog's skin and drink the blood. Their only food and drink is dog's blood. Dogs can get Lyme disease, Rocky Mountain spotted fever (normally found in the US only), paralysis and many other diseases from ticks and mites. They may live where fleas are found and they like to hide in

The head of a dog tick, *Dermacentor variabilis*, enlarged and coloured for effect.

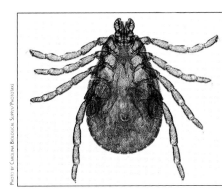

PHOTO BY CAROLINA BIOLOGICAL SUPPLY/PHOTOTAKE

A brown dog tick, *Rhipicephalus sanguineus*, is an uncommon but annoying tick found on dogs.

cracks or seams in walls wherever dogs live. They are controlled the same way fleas are controlled.

The dog tick, *Dermacentor variabilis*, may well be the most common dog tick in many geographical areas, especially those areas where the climate is hot and humid.

DEER TICK CROSSING

The great outdoors may be fun for your dog, but it also is a home to dangerous ticks. Deer ticks carry a bacterium known as *Borrelia burgdorferi* and are most active in the autumn and spring. When infections are caught early, penicillin and tetracycline are effective antibiotics, but if left untreated the bacteria may cause neurological, kidney and cardiac problems as well as long-term trouble with walking and painful joints.

Human lice look like dog lice; the two are closely related.

Most dog ticks have life expectancies of a week to six months, depending upon climatic conditions. They can neither jump nor fly, but they can crawl slowly and can range up to 5 metres (16 feet) to reach a sleeping or unsuspecting dog.

MANGE

Mites cause a skin irritation called mange. Some are contagious, like *Cheyletiella*, ear mites, scabies and chiggers. Mites that cause ear-mite infestations are usually controlled with Lindane, which can only be

Opposite page:
The dog tick, *Dermacentor variabilis*, is probably the most common tick found on dogs. Look at the strength in its eight legs! No wonder it's hard to detach them.

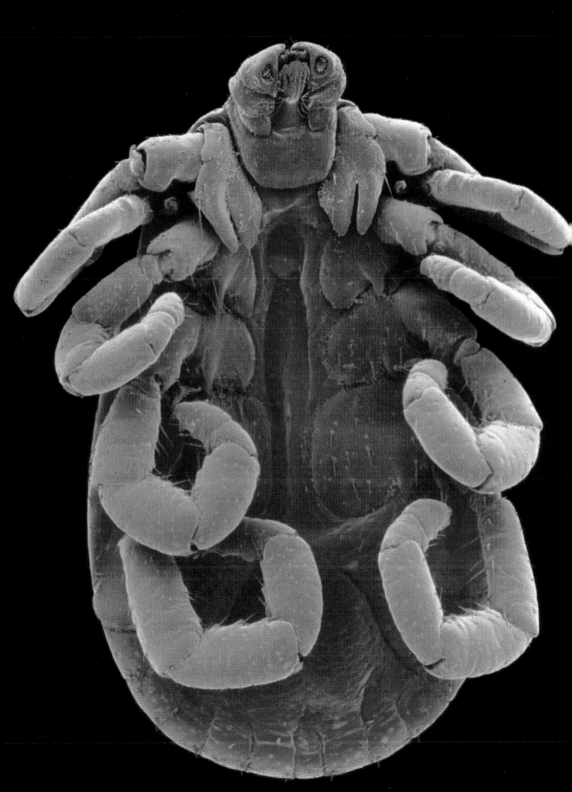

The roundworm, *Rhabditis*. The roundworm can infect both dogs and humans.

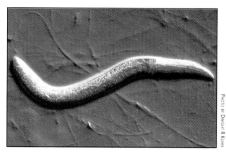

The common roundworm, *Ascaris lumbricoides*.

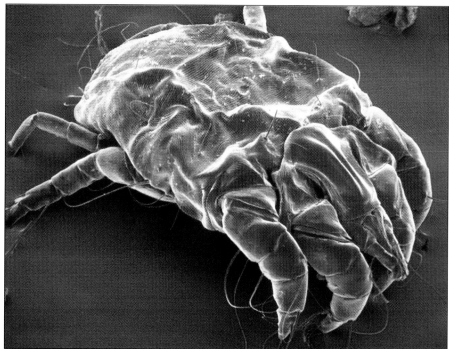

The mange mite, *Psoroptes bovis*.

administered by a vet, followed by Tresaderm at home.

It is essential that your dog be treated for mange as quickly as possible because some forms of mange are transmissible to people.

INTERNAL PARASITES

Most animals—fishes, birds and mammals, including dogs and humans—have worms and other parasites that live inside their bodies. According to Dr Herbert R Axelrod, the fish pathologist, there are two kinds of parasites: dumb and smart. The smart parasites live in peaceful cooperation with their hosts (symbiosis), while the dumb parasites kill their hosts. Most of the worm infections are relatively easy to control. If they are not controlled, they weaken the host dog to the point that other medical problems occur, but they are not dumb parasites.

ROUNDWORMS

The roundworms that infect dogs are scientifically known as *Toxocara canis*. They live in the dog's intestines. The worms shed eggs continually. It has been estimated that a dog produces about 150 grammes of faeces every day. Each gramme of faeces

ROUNDWORMS

Average-size dogs can pass 1,360,000 roundworm eggs every day. For example, if there were only 1 million dogs in the world, the world would be saturated with 1,300 metric tonnes of dog faeces. These faeces would contain 15,000,000,000 roundworm eggs.

Up to 31% of home gardens and children's play boxes in the US contain roundworm eggs.

Flushing dog's faeces down the toilet is not a safe practice because the usual sewage treatments do not destroy roundworm eggs.

Infected puppies start shedding roundworm eggs at 3 weeks of age. They can be infected by their mother's milk.

DEWORMING

Ridding your puppy of worms is *very important* because certain worms that puppies carry, such as tapeworms and roundworms, can infect humans.

Breeders initiate deworming programmes at or about four weeks of age. The routine is repeated every two or three weeks until the puppy is three months old. The breeder from whom you obtained your puppy should provide you with the complete details of the deworming programme.

Your veterinary surgeon can prescribe and monitor the programme of deworming for you. The usual programme is treating the puppy every 15–20 days until the puppy is positively worm-free. It is advised that you only treat your puppy with drugs that are recommended professionally.

averages 10,000–12,000 eggs of roundworms. There are no known areas in which dogs roam that do not contain roundworm eggs. The greatest danger of roundworms is that they infect people too! It is wise to have your dog tested regularly for roundworms.

Pigs also have roundworm infections that can be passed to humans and dogs. The typical roundworm parasite is called *Ascaris lumbricoides*.

The roundworm *Rhabditis.*

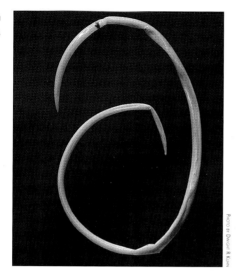

PHOTO BY DWIGHT R KUHN

preventative in Collies, can be used for this purpose.

In Britain the 'temperate climate' hookworm (*Uncinaria stenocephala*) is rarely found in pet or show dogs, but can occur in hunting packs, racing Greyhounds and sheepdogs because the worms can be prevalent wherever dogs are exercised regularly on grassland.

TAPEWORMS

There are many species of tapeworm. They are carried by fleas! The dog eats the flea and starts the tapeworm cycle. Humans can also be infected with tapeworms, so don't eat fleas! Fleas are so small that your dog could pass them onto your hands, your plate or your food and thus make it possible for you to ingest a flea that is carrying tapeworm eggs.

While tapeworm infection is

HOOKWORMS

Right: Male and female hookworms. *Ancylostoma caninum* are uncommonly found in pet or show dogs in Britain.

Below: The infective stage of the hookworm larva.

The worm *Ancylostoma caninum* is commonly called the dog hookworm. It is also dangerous to humans and cats. It has teeth by which it attaches itself to the intestines of the dog. It changes the site of its attachment about six times a day and the dog loses blood from each detachment, possibly causing iron-deficiency anaemia. Hookworms are easily purged from the dog with many medications. Milbemycin oxime, which also serves as a heartworm

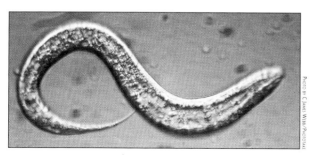

PHOTO BY C JAMES WEBB / PHOTOTAKE

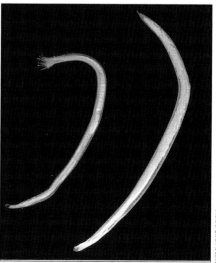

PHOTO BY DWIGHT R KUHN

Heartworm, *Dirofilaria immitis.*

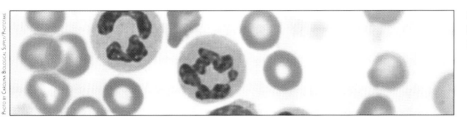

Magnified heartworm larvae, *Dirofilaria immitis.*

not life-threatening in dogs (smart parasite!), it can be the cause of a very serious liver disease for humans. About 50 percent of the humans infected with *Echinococcus multilocularis*, a type of tapeworm that causes alveolar hydatis, perish.

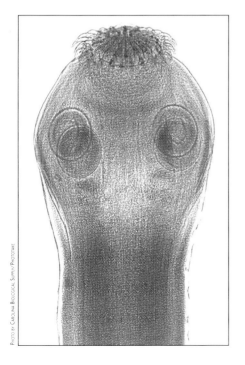

TAPEWORMS

Humans, rats, squirrels, foxes, coyotes, wolves, and domestic dogs are all susceptible to tapeworm infection. Except in humans, tapeworms are usually not a fatal infection. Infected individuals can harbour a thousand parasitic worms.

Tapeworms have two sexes—male and female (many other worms have only one sex—male and female in the same worm).

If dogs eat infected rats or mice, they get the tapeworm disease. One month after attaching to a dog's intestine, the worm starts shedding eggs. These eggs are infective immediately. Infective eggs can live for a few months without a host animal.

The head and rostellum (the round prominence on the scolex) of a tapeworm, which infects dogs and humans.

First Aid at a Glance

Burns
Place the affected area under cool water; use ice if only a small area is burnt.

Bee/Insect bites
Apply ice to relieve swelling; antihistamine dosed properly.

Animal bites
Clean any bleeding area; apply pressure until bleeding subsides; go to the vet.

Spider bites
Use cold compress and a pressurised pack to inhibit venom's spreading.

Antifreeze poisoning
Induce vomiting with hydrogen peroxide. Seek *immediate* veterinary help!

Fish hooks
Removal best handled by vet; hook must be cut in order to remove.

Snake bites
Pack ice around bite; contact vet quickly; identify snake for proper antivenin.

Car accident
Move dog from roadway with blanket; seek veterinary aid.

Shock
Calm the dog, keep him warm; seek immediate veterinary help.

Nosebleed
Apply cold compress to the nose; apply pressure to any visible abrasion.

Bleeding
Apply pressure above the area; treat wound by applying a cotton pack.

Heat stroke
Submerge dog in cold bath; cool down with fresh air and water; go to the vet.

Frostbite/Hypothermia
Warm the dog with a warm bath, electric blankets or hot water bottles.

Abrasions
Clean the wound and wash out thoroughly with fresh water; apply antiseptic.

 Remember: an injured dog may attempt to bite a helping hand from fear and confusion. Always muzzle the dog before trying to offer assistance.

HEARTWORMS

Heartworms are thin, extended worms up to 30 cms (12 ins) long, which live in a dog's heart and the major blood vessels surrounding it. Dogs may have up to 200 worms. Symptoms may be loss of energy, loss of appetite, coughing, the development of a pot belly and anaemia.

Heartworms are transmitted by mosquitoes. The mosquito drinks the blood of an infected dog and takes in larvae with the blood. The larvae, called microfilaria, develop within the body of the mosquito and are passed on to the next dog bitten after the larvae mature. It takes two to three weeks for the larvae to develop to the infective stage within the body of the mosquito. Dogs should be treated at about six weeks of age, and maintained on a prophylactic dose given monthly.

Blood testing for heartworms is not necessarily indicative of how seriously your dog is infected. This is a dangerous disease. Although heartworm is a problem for dogs in America, Australia, Asia and Central Europe, dogs in the United Kingdom are not currently affected by heartworm.

The heart of a dog infected with canine heartworm, *Dirofilaria immitis.*

HOMEOPATHY:
an alternative to conventional medicine

'Less is Most'

Using this principle, the strength of a homeopathic remedy is measured by the number of serial dilutions that were undertaken to create it. The greater the number of serial dilutions, the greater the strength of the homeopathic remedy. The potency of a remedy that has been made by making a dilution of 1 part in 100 parts (or 1/100) is 1c or 1cH. If this remedy is subjected to a series of further dilutions, each one being 1/100, a more dilute and stronger remedy is produced. If the remedy is diluted in this way six times, it is called 6c or 6cH. A dilution of 6c is 1 part in 1,000,000,000,000. In general, higher potencies in more frequent doses are better for acute symptoms and lower potencies in more infrequent doses are more useful for chronic, long-standing problems.

CURING OUR DOGS NATURALLY

Holistic medicine means treating the whole animal as a unique, perfect living being. Generally, holistic treatments do not suppress the symptoms that the body naturally produces, as do most medications prescribed by conventional doctors and vets. Holistic methods seek to cure disease by regaining balance and harmony in the patient's environment. Some of these methods include use of nutritional therapy, herbs, flower essences, aromatherapy, acupuncture, massage, chiropractic and, of course, the most popular holistic approach, homeopathy.

Homeopathy is a theory or system of treating illness with small doses of substances which, if administered in larger quantities, would produce the symptoms that the patient already has. This approach is often described as 'like cures like.' Although modern veterinary medicine is geared toward the 'quick fix,' homeopathy relies on the belief that, given the time, the body is able to heal itself and return to its natural, healthy state.

Choosing a remedy to cure a problem in our dogs is the difficult part of homeopathy. Consult with your veterinary surgeon for a professional diagnosis of your dog's symptoms. Often these symptoms require immediate conventional care. If your vet is willing, and knowledgeable, you may attempt a homeopathic remedy. Be aware that cortisone prevents homeopathic remedies from working. There are hundreds of possibilities and combinations to cure many problems in dogs, from basic physical problems such as excessive moulting, fleas or other parasites, unattractive doggy odour, bad breath, upset tummy, obesity, dry, oily or dull coat, diarrhoea, ear problems or eye discharge (including tears and dry or mucousy matter), to behavioural abnormalities, such as fear of loud noises, habitual licking, poor appetite, excessive barking and various phobias. From alumina to zincum metallicum, the remedies span the planet and the imagination…from flowers and weeds to chemicals, insect droppings, diesel smoke and volcanic ash.

Using 'Like to Treat Like'

Unlike conventional medicines that suppress symptoms, homeopathic remedies treat illnesses with small doses of substances that, if administered in larger quantities, would produce the symptoms that the patient already has. While the same homeopathic remedy can be used to treat different symptoms in different dogs, here are some interesting remedies and their uses.

Apis Mellifica
(made from honey bee venom) can be used for allergies or to reduce swelling that occurs in acutely infected kidneys.

Diesel Smoke
can be used to help control travel sickness.

Calcarea Fluorica
(made from calcium fluoride, which helps harden bone structure) can be useful in treating hard lumps in tissues.

Natrum Muriaticum
(made from common salt, sodium chloride) is useful in treating thin, thirsty dogs.

Nitricum Acidum
(made from nitric acid) is used for symptoms you would expect to see from contact with acids, such as lesions, especially where the skin joins the linings of body orifices or openings such as the lips and nostrils.

Symphytum
(made from the herb Knitbone, *Symphytum officianale*) is used to encourage bones to heal.

Urtica Urens
(made from the common stinging nettle) is used in treating painful, irritating rashes.

HOMEOPATHIC REMEDIES FOR YOUR DOG

Symptom/Ailment	Possible Remedy
ALLERGIES	Apis Mellifica 30c, Astacus Fluviatilis 6c, Pulsatilla 30c, Urtica Urens 6c
ALOPAECIA	Alumina 30c, Lycopodium 30c, Sepia 30c, Thallium 6c
ANAL GLANDS (BLOCKED)	Hepar Sulphuris Calcareum 30c, Sanicula 6c, Silicea 6c
ARTHRITIS	Rhus Toxicodendron 6c, Bryonia Alba 6c
CATARACT	Calcarea Carbonica 6c, Conium Maculatum 6c, Phosphorus 30c, Silicea 30c
CONSTIPATION	Alumina 6c, Carbo Vegetabilis 30c, Graphites 6c, Nitricum Acidum 30c, Silicea 6c
COUGHING	Aconitum Napellus 6c, Belladonna 30c, Hyoscyamus Niger 30c, Phosphorus 30c
DIARRHOEA	Arsenicum Album 30c, Aconitum Napellus 6c, Chamomilla 30c, Mercurius Corrosivus 30c
DRY EYE	Zincum Metallicum 30c
EAR PROBLEMS	Aconitum Napellus 30c, Belladonna 30c, Hepar Sulphuris 30c, Tellurium 30c, Psorinum 200c
EYE PROBLEMS	Borax 6c, Aconitum Napellus 30c, Graphites 6c, Staphysagria 6c, Thuja Occidentalis 30c
GLAUCOMA	Aconitum Napellus 30c, Apis Mellifica 6c, Phosphorus 30c
HEAT STROKE	Belladonna 30c, Gelsemium Sempervirens 30c, Sulphur 30c
HICCOUGHS	Cinchona Deficinalis 6c
HIP DYSPLASIA	Colocynthis 6c, Rhus Toxicodendron 6c, Bryonia Alba 6c
INCONTINENCE	Argentum Nitricum 6c, Causticum 30c, Conium Maculatum 30c, Pulsatilla 30c, Sepia 30c
INSECT BITES	Apis Mellifica 30c, Cantharis 30c, Hypericum Perforatum 6c, Urtica Urens 30c
ITCHING	Alumina 30c, Arsenicum Album 30c, Carbo Vegetabilis 30c, Hypericum Perforatum 6c, Mezerium 6c, Sulphur 30c
KENNEL COUGH	Drosera 6c, Ipecacuanha 30c
MASTITIS	Apis Mellifica 30c, Belladonna 30c, Urtica Urens 1m
PATELLAR LUXATION	Gelsemium Sempervirens 6c, Rhus Toxicodendron 6c
PENIS PROBLEMS	Aconitum Napellus 30c, Hepar Sulphuris Calcareum 30c, Pulsatilla 30c, Thuja Occidentalis 6c
PUPPY TEETHING	Calcarea Carbonica 6c, Chamomilla 6c, Phytolacca 6c
TRAVEL SICKNESS	Cocculus 6c, Petroleum 6c

Recognising a Sick Dog

Unlike colicky babies and cranky children, our canine charges cannot tell us when they are feeling ill. Therefore, there are a number of signs that owners can identify to know that their dogs are not feeling well.

Take note for physical manifestations such as:

- unusual, bad odour, including bad breath
- excessive moulting
- wax in the ears, chronic ear irritation
- oily, flaky, dull haircoat
- mucous, tearing or similar discharge in the eyes
- fleas or mites
- mucous in stool, diarrhoea
- sensitivity to petting or handling
- licking at paws, scratching face, etc.

Keep an eye out for behavioural changes as well including:

- lethargy, idleness
- lack of patience or general irritability
- lack of appetite, digestive problems
- phobias (fear of people, loud noises, etc.)
- strange behaviour, suspicion, fear
- coprophagia
- more frequent barking
- whimpering, crying

Get Well Soon

You don't need a DVR or a BVMA to provide good TLC to your sick or recovering dog, but you do need to pay attention to some details that normally wouldn't bother him. The following tips will aid Fido's recovery and get him back on his paws again:

- Keep his space free of irritating smells, like heavy perfumes and air fresheners.
- Rest is the best medicine! Avoid harsh lighting that will prevent your dog from sleeping. Shade him from bright sunlight during the day and dim the lights in the evening.
- Keep the noise level down. Animals are more sensitive to sound when they are sick.

- Be attentive to any necessary temperature adjustments. A dog with a fever needs a cool room and cold liquids. A bitch that is whelping or recovering from surgery will be more comfortable in a warm room, consuming warm liquids and food.
- You wouldn't send a sick child back to school early, so don't rush your dog back into a full routine until he seems absolutely ready.

The term *old* is a qualitative term. For dogs, as well as their masters, old is relative. Certainly we can all distinguish between a puppy Chinese Crested and an adult Chinese Crested—there are the obvious physical traits, such as size, appearance and facial expressions, and personality traits. Puppies and young dogs like to play with children. Children's natural exuberance is a good match for the seemingly endless energy of young dogs. They like to run, jump, chase and retrieve. On the other hand, if a Chinese Crested is only exposed to people over 60 years of age, its life will normally be less active and it will not seem to be getting old as its activity level slows down.

If people live to be 100 years old, dogs live to be 20 years old. While this is a good rule of thumb, it is very inaccurate. When trying to compare dog years to human years, you cannot make a generalisation about all dogs. You can make the generalisation that 13–14 years is a good lifespan for a Chinese Crested, but some can live even longer. This is a rather long lifespan, as small dogs generally live longer than large breeds. Dogs are generally considered mature at three years of age, but can reproduce even earlier. So the first three years of a dog's life are like seven times that of comparable humans. That means a 3-year-old dog is like a 21-year-old human. As the curve of comparison shows, there is no hard and fast rule for comparing dog and human ages. The comparison is made even more difficult, for not all humans age at the same rate...and human females live longer than human males. A Chinese Crested can be considered a senior by the time his is seven years of age.

WHAT TO LOOK FOR IN SENIORS

Most veterinary surgeons and behaviourists use the seventh-year mark as the time to consider a dog a 'senior.' The term 'senior' does not imply that the dog is geriatric and has begun to fail in mind and body. Ageing is essentially a slowing process. Humans readily admit that they feel a difference in their activity level from age 20 to 30, and then from 30 to 40, etc. By treating the

CDS: COGNITIVE DYSFUNCTION SYNDROME
'OLD-DOG SYNDROME'

There are many ways to evaluate old-dog syndrome. Veterinary surgeons have defined CDS (cognitive dysfunction syndrome) as the gradual deterioration of cognitive abilities. These are indicated by changes in the dog's behaviour. When a dog changes its routine response, and maladies have been eliminated as the cause of these behavioural changes, then CDS is the usual diagnosis.

More than half the dogs over eight years old suffer from some form of CDS. The older the dog, the more chance it has of suffering from CDS. In humans, doctors often dismiss the CDS behavioural changes as part of 'winding down.'

There are four major signs of CDS: the dog has frequent toilet accidents inside the home, sleeps much more or much less than normal, acts confused and fails to respond to social stimuli.

SYMPTOMS OF CDS

FREQUENT TOILET ACCIDENTS
- *Urinates in the house.*
- *Defecates in the house.*
- *Doesn't signal that he wants to go out.*

SLEEP PATTERNS
- *Moves much more slowly.*
- *Sleeps more than normal during the day.*
- *Sleeps less during the night.*

CONFUSION
- *Goes outside and just stands there.*
- *Appears confused with a faraway look in his eyes.*
- *Hides more often.*
- *Doesn't recognise friends.*
- *Doesn't come when called.*
- *Walks around listlessly and without a destination.*

FAILS TO RESPOND TO SOCIAL STIMULI
- *Comes to people less frequently, whether called or not.*
- *Doesn't tolerate petting for more than a short time.*
- *Doesn't come to the door when you return home.*

seven-year-old dog as a senior, owners are able to implement certain therapeutic and preventative medical strategies with the help of their veterinary surgeons. A senior-care programme should include at least two veterinary visits per year, screening sessions to determine the dog's health status, as well as nutritional counselling. Veterinary surgeons determine the senior dog's health status through a blood smear for a complete blood count, serum chemistry profile with electrolytes, urinalysis, blood pressure check, electrocardiogram, ocular tonometry (pressure on the eyeball) and dental prophylaxis.

Such an extensive programme for senior dogs is well advised before owners start to see the obvious physical signs of ageing, such as slower and inhibited movement, wrinkles, increased sleep/nap periods and disinterest in play and other activity. This preventative programme promises a longer, healthier life for the ageing dog. Among the physical problems common in ageing dogs are the loss of sight and hearing, arthritis, kidney and liver failure, diabetes mellitus, heart disease and Cushing's disease (a hormonal disease).

In addition to the physical manifestations discussed, there are some behavioural changes and problems related to ageing dogs. Dogs suffering from hearing

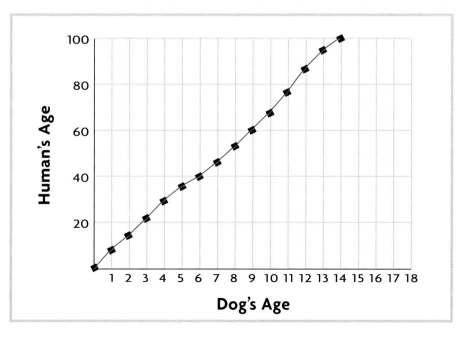

or vision loss, dental discomfort or arthritis can become aggressive. Likewise the near-deaf and/or blind dog may be startled more easily and react in an unexpectedly aggressive manner. Seniors suffering from senility can become more impatient and irritable. Housesoiling accidents are associated with loss of mobility, kidney problems and loss of sphincter control as well as plaque accumulation, physiological brain changes and reactions to medications. Older dogs, just like young puppies, suffer from separation anxiety, which can lead to excessive barking, whining, housesoiling and destructive behaviour. Seniors may become fearful of everyday sounds, such as vacuum cleaners, heaters, thunder and passing traffic. Some dogs have difficulty sleeping, due to discomfort, the need for frequent toilet visits and the like.

Owners should avoid spoiling the older dog with too many fatty treats. Obesity is a common problem in older dogs and subtracts years from their lives. Keep the senior dog as trim as possible since excessive weight puts additional stress on the body's vital organs. Some breeders recommend supplementing the diet with foods high in fibre and lower in calories. Adding fresh vegetables and marrow broth to the senior's diet makes a tasty, low-calorie, low-fat supplement. Vets also offer speciality diets for senior dogs that are worth exploring.

Your dog, as he nears his twilight years, needs his owner's patience and good care more than ever. Never punish an older dog for an accident or abnormal behaviour. For all the years of love, protection and companionship that your dog has provided, he deserves special attention and courtesies. The older dog may need to relieve himself at 3 a.m. because he can no longer hold it for eight hours. Older dogs may not be able to remain crated for more than two or three hours. It may be time to give up a sofa or chair to your old friend. Although he may not seem as enthusiastic about your attention and petting, he does appreciate the considerations you offer as he gets older.

Your Chinese Crested does not understand why his world is slowing down. Owners must make the transition into the golden years as pleasant and rewarding as possible.

WHAT TO DO WHEN THE TIME COMES

You are never fully prepared to make a rational decision about putting your dog to sleep. It is very obvious that you love your Chinese Crested or you would not be reading this book. Putting a loved dog to sleep is extremely difficult. It is a decision that must be made with your veterinary surgeon. You are usually forced to make the decision when one of the life-threatening symptoms listed above becomes serious enough for you to seek medical (veterinary) help.

If the prognosis of the malady indicates the end is near and your beloved pet will only suffer more and experience no enjoyment for the balance of its life, then euthanasia is the right choice.

WHAT IS EUTHANASIA?
Euthanasia derives from the Greek, meaning *good death*. In other words, it means the planned, painless killing of a dog suffering from a painful, incurable condition, or who is so aged that it cannot walk, see, eat or control its excretory functions.

Euthanasia is usually accomplished by injection with an overdose of an anaesthesia or barbiturate. Aside from the prick of the needle, the experience is usually painless.

MAKING THE DECISION
The decision to euthanise your dog is never easy. The days during which the dog becomes ill and the end occurs can be unusually stressful for you. If this is your first experience with the death of a loved one, you may need the comfort dictated by

your religious beliefs. If you are the head of the family and have children, you should have involved them in the decision of putting your Chinese Crested to sleep. Usually your dog can be maintained on drugs for a few days in order to give you ample time to make a decision. During this time, talking with members of your family or even people who have lived through this same experience can ease the burden of your inevitable decision.

THE FINAL RESTING PLACE
Dogs can have some of the same privileges as humans. The remains of your beloved dog can be buried in a pet cemetery, which is generally expensive. Dogs who have died at home can be buried in your garden in a place suitably marked with some stone or newly planted tree or bush. Alternatively, they can be cremated individually and the ashes returned to you. A less expensive option is mass cremation, although, of course, the ashes can not then be returned. Vets can usually arrange the cremation on your behalf. The cost of these options should always be discussed frankly and openly with your veterinary surgeon. In Britain if your dog has died at the surgery, the vet legally cannot allow you to take your dog's body home.

Showing Your
CHINESE CRESTED

When you purchased your Chinese Crested you should have made it clear to the breeder whether you wanted one just as a loveable companion and pet, or if you hoped to be buying a Chinese Crested with show prospects. No reputable breeder will sell you a young puppy saying that it is *definitely* of show quality, for so much can go wrong during the early months of a puppy's development. If you plan to show, what you will hopefully have acquired is a puppy with 'show potential.'

To the novice, exhibiting a Chinese Crested in the show ring may look easy but it takes a lot of hard work and devotion to do top winning at a show such as the prestigious Crufts, not to mention a little luck too!

The first concept that the canine novice learns when watching a dog show is that each dog first competes against members of its own breed. Once the judge has selected the best member of each breed, provided that the show is judged on a Group system, that chosen dog will compete with other dogs in its group. Finally the best of each group will compete for Best in Show and Reserve Best in Show.

The second concept that you must understand is that the dogs are not actually compared against one another. The judge compares each dog against the breed standard, which is a written description of the ideal specimen of the breed. While some early

INFORMATION ON SHOWS

You can get information about dog shows from kennel clubs and breed clubs:

Fédération Cynologique Internationale
14, rue Leopold II, B-6530 Thuin, Belgium
www.fci.be

The Kennel Club
1-5 Clarges Street, Piccadilly,
London W1Y 8AB, UK
www.the-kennel-club.org.uk

American Kennel Club
5580 Centerview Drive,
Raleigh, NC 27606-3390 USA
www.akc.org

Canadian Kennel Club
89 Skyway Ave., Suite 100, Etobicoke,
Ontario
M9W 6R4 Canada
www.ckc.ca

breed standards were indeed based on specific dogs that were famous or popular, many dedicated enthusiasts say that a perfect specimen, described in the standard, has never walked into a show ring, has never been bred and, to the woe of dog breeders around the globe, does not exist. Breeders attempt to get as close to this ideal as possible, with every litter, but theoretically the 'perfect' dog is so elusive that it is impossible. (And if the 'perfect' dog were born, breeders and judges would never agree that it was indeed 'perfect.')

If you are interested in exploring dog shows, your best bet is to join your local breed club. These clubs often host both Championship and Open Shows, and sometimes Match meetings and special events, all of which could be of interest, even if you are only an onlooker. Clubs also send out newsletters and some organise training days and seminars in order that people may learn more about their chosen breed. To locate the breed club closest to you, contact The Kennel Club, the ruling body for the British dog world. The Kennel Club governs not only conformation shows but also working trials, obedience shows, agility trials and field trials. The Kennel Club furnishes the rules and regulations for all these events plus general dog registration and other

HOW TO ENTER A DOG SHOW

1. Obtain an entry form and show schedule from the Show Secretary.
2. Select the classes that you want to enter and complete the entry form.
3. Transfer your dog into your name at The Kennel Club. (Be sure that this matter is handled before entering.)
4. Find out how far in advance show entries must be made. Oftentimes it's more than a couple of months.

basic requirements of dog ownership. Its annual show, called the Crufts Dog Show, held in Birmingham, is the largest benched show in England. Every year over 20,000 of the UK's best dogs qualify to participate in this marvellous show, which lasts four days.

The Kennel Club governs many different kinds of shows in Great Britain, Australia, South Africa and beyond. At the most competitive and prestigious of these shows, the Championship Shows, a dog can earn Challenge Certificates (CCs), and thereby become a Show Champion or a Champion. A dog must earn three Challenge Certificates under three different judges to earn the prefix of 'Sh Ch' or 'Ch.' Note that some breeds must also qualify in a field trial in order to gain the title of full champion, though, of course, the Chinese Crested is not such a breed. Challenge Certificates are awarded to a very small percentage of the dogs competing, and dogs that are already Champions compete with others for these coveted CCs. The number of Challenge Certificates awarded in any one year is based upon the total number of dogs in each breed entered for competition.

There are three types of Championship Shows: an all-breed General Championship

The start of a promising career... Pictured here winning Best Puppy at a South Wales Kennel Association show, this bitch went on to become a champion.

Each dog takes a
turn around the
ring as the judge
evaluates the
dog's movement.

Show for all Kennel-Club-recognised breeds; a Group Championship Show that is limited to breeds within one of the groups; and a Breed Show that is usually confined to a single breed. The Kennel Club determines which breeds at which Championship Shows will have the opportunity to earn Challenge Certificates (or tickets). Serious exhibitors often will opt not to participate if the tickets are withheld at a particular show. This policy makes earning championships even more difficult to accomplish.

Open Shows are generally less competitive and are frequently used as 'practice shows' for young

Each dog takes a turn around the ring as the judge evaluates the dog's movement.

Behind the scenes... A Powder Puff awaits 'show time' after a last-minute touch-up in the grooming area.

dogs. There are hundreds of Open Shows each year that can be delightful social events and are great first show experiences for the novice. Even if you're considering just watching a show to wet your paws, an Open Show is a great choice.

While Championship and Open Shows are most important for the beginner to understand, there are other types of shows in which the interested dog owner can participate. Training clubs sponsor Matches that can be entered on the day of the show for a nominal fee. In these introductory-level exhibitions, two dogs are pulled out of a hat and 'matched,' the winner of that match goes on to the next round, and eventually only one dog is left undefeated.

Exemption Shows are much more light-hearted affairs with usually only four pedigree classes and several 'fun' classes, all of which can be entered on the day of the show. Exemption Shows are sometimes held in conjunction with small agricultural shows and the proceeds must be given to a charity. Limited Shows are also available in small number, but entry is restricted to members of the club which hosts the show, although one can usually join the club when making an entry.

Before you actually step into the ring, you would be well advised to sit back and observe the judge's ring procedure. If it is your first time in the ring, do not be over-anxious and run to the front of the line. It is much better to stand back and study how the exhibitor in front of you is performing. The judge asks each handler to 'stand' the dog, hopefully showing the dog off to his best advantage. The judge will observe the dog from a distance and from different angles, approach the dog, check his teeth, overall structure, alertness and muscle tone, as well as consider how well the dog 'conforms' to the standard. Most importantly, the judge will have the exhibitor move the dog around the ring in some pattern that he or she should specify (another advantage to not going first, but always listen

A small breed like the Chinese Crested is examined on a table so that the judge can get a closer look.

since some judges change their directions, and the judge is always right!). Finally the judge will give the dog one last look before moving on to the next exhibitor.

If you are not in the top three at your first show, do not be discouraged. Be patient and consistent and you may eventually find yourself in the winning line-up. Remember that the winners were once in your shoes and have devoted many hours and much money to earn the placement. If you find that your dog is losing every time and never getting a nod, it may be time to consider a different dog sport or just enjoy your Chinese Crested as a pet.

AGILITY TRIALS

Agility trials began in the United Kingdom in 1977 and have since spread around the world, especially to the United States, where they are very popular. The handler directs his dog over an obstacle course that includes jumps (such as those used in the working trials), as well as tyres, the dog walk, weave poles, pipe tunnels, collapsed tunnels, etc. Some Chinese Cresteds do participate in mini-agility, which is basically the same, except the obstacles have been reduced in size. The Kennel Club requires that dogs not be trained for agility until they are 12 months old. This dog sport is great fun for dog and

DID YOU KNOW?

The FCI *does not* issue pedigrees. The FCI members and contract partners are responsible for issuing pedigrees and training judges in their own countries. The FCI does maintain a list of judges and makes sure that they are recognised throughout the FCI member countries.

The FCI also *does not* act as a breeder referral; breeder information is available from FCI-recognised national canine societies in each of the FCI's member countries.

owner, and interested owners should join a training club that has obstacles and experienced agility handlers who can introduce you and your dog to the 'ropes' (and tyres, tunnels, etc.).

FÉDÉRATION CYNOLOGIQUE INTERNATIONALE

Established in 1911, the Fédération Cynologique Internationale (FCI) represents the 'world kennel club.' This international body brings uniformity to the breeding, judging and showing of pure-bred dogs. Although the FCI originally included only five European nations: France, Germany, Austria, the Netherlands and Belgium (which remains its headquarters), the organisation today embraces nations on six continents and recognises well over 300 breeds of pure-bred dog.

There are three titles attainable through the FCI: the International Champion, which is the most prestigious; the International Beauty Champion, which is based on aptitude certificates in different countries; and the International Trial Champion, which is based on achievement in obedience trials in different countries

FCI sponsors both national and international shows. The hosting country determines the judging system and breed standards are always based on the breed's country of origin. Dogs from every country can participate in these impressive canine spectacles, the largest of which is the World Dog Show, hosted in a different country each year.

The FCI is divided into ten 'groups.' At the World Dog Show, the following 'classes' are offered for each breed: Puppy Class (6–9 months), Youth Class (9–18 months), Open Class (15 months or older) and Champion Class. A dog can be awarded a classification of Excellent, Very Good, Good, Sufficient and Not Sufficient. Puppies can be awarded classifications of Very Promising, Promising or Not Promising. Four placements are made in each class. After all sexes and classes are judged, a Best of Breed is selected. Other special groups and classes may also be shown. Each exhibitor showing a dog receives a written evaluation from the judge.

Besides the World Dog Show, you can exhibit your dog at speciality shows held by different breed clubs. Speciality shows may have their own regulations.

FCI INFORMATION

There are 330 breeds recognised by the FCI, and each breed is considered to be 'owned' by a specific country. Each breed standard is a cooperative effort between the breed's country and the FCI's Standards and Scientific Commissions. Judges use these official breed standards at shows held in FCI member countries. One of the functions of the FCI is to update and translate the breed standards into French, English, Spanish and German.

INDEX

My Chinese Crested

PUT YOUR PUPPY'S FIRST PICTURE HERE

Dog's Name _____

Date _____ Photographer _____